THE
DE COSMOS
ENIGMA

THE
De Cosmos
ENIGMA

GORDON HAWKINS

RONSDALE PRESS

THE DE COSMOS ENIGMA
Copyright © 2015 Gordon Hawkins

RONSDALE PRESS
3350 West 21st Avenue, Vancouver, B.C. Canada V6S 1G7
www.ronsdalepress.com

Typesetting: Julie Cochrane, in Horley 11.5 pt on 17
Cover Design: Julie Cochrane
Cover Photo: Amor De Cosmos, c. 1874, BCPA, C-06116
Index: Meagan Dyer
Paper: Ancient Forest Friendly Rolland 60 lb. Opaque, FSC Recycled,
    100% post-consumer waste, totally chlorine-free and acid-free.

Ronsdale Press wishes to thank the following for their support of its publishing
program: the Canada Council for the Arts, the Government of Canada through the
Canada Book Fund, the British Columbia Arts Council, and the Province of British
Columbia through the British Columbia Book Publishing Tax Credit program.

Library and Archives Canada Cataloguing in Publication

Hawkins, Gordon, 1921–, author
    The De Cosmos enigma / Gordon Hawkins.

Includes bibliographical references and index.
Issued in print and electronic formats.
ISBN 978-1-55380-353-9 (print)
ISBN 978-1-55380-354-6 (ebook) / ISBN 978-1-55380-355-3 (pdf)

    1. De Cosmos, Amor, 1825-1897. 2. Journalists—British Columbia—Biography.
3. Politicians—British Columbia—Biography. 4. British Columbia—Politics and
government—1849–1871. 5. British Columbia—Politics and government—
1871 1903. I. Title.

FC3823.1.D4H39 2015   971.1'02092   C2014-907029-2   C2014-907030-6

At Ronsdale Press we are committed to protecting the environment. To this end we
are working with Canopy (formerly Markets Initiative) and printers to phase out our
use of paper produced from ancient forests. This book is one step towards that goal.

Printed in Canada by Marquis Book Printing, Quebec

To my daughter Rosalind,
in appreciation of your
advice and encouragement
in this project

"... *Mind and motive are only
explicable from what appears to reflect
them and, in respect of such subtle
and elusive but basic elements of history,
we can never be sure that our analyses
are not at fault. . . .*"

— R. E. GOSNELL, Preface to Part Two of
British Columbia, Sixty Years of Progress, 1913

ACKNOWLEDGEMENTS

In addition to the encouragement and tolerance of family and friends, especially Martine Gow-Cooper, my greatest debts are to the helpful staff and the facilities of the Public Archives of British Columbia, the Central Branch of the Greater Victoria Public Library (with its invaluable Heritage Room) and, throughout the whole project, to the oversight and editorial guidance of Ronald Hatch and Meagan Dyer at Ronsdale Press.

CONTENTS

INTRODUCTION   The Quest / 11

CHAPTER 1   Halifax / 15

CHAPTER 2   Westward / 25

CHAPTER 3   The Transformation / 35

CHAPTER 4   The Transition / 45

CHAPTER 5   Victoria: Business Strategies / 53

CHAPTER 6   The Newspaperman / 61

CHAPTER 7   Entering the Political Arena / 73

CHAPTER 8   The Great Campaigner: Triumphs
             and Disappointments / 99

CHAPTER 9   A Summing Up / 141

Notes / 153

Select Bibliography / 161

About the Author / 165

Index / 167

The Quest

At his interment in Victoria's Ross Bay Cemetery, the coffin was bare. There was no eulogy, no music and only a meagre gathering of mourners. John Helmcken, his long-time adversary, called the event "a mockery of honour." Never again, he wrote, "would a man be laid away in the cold-blooded fashion in which he was consigned to the grave by a people who owed him so much."[1]

Helmcken was writing of Amor De Cosmos, the man who had played a critical, if controversial role in the union of Vancouver Island with mainland British Columbia and had campaigned hard and, in the end, successfully, for the new province's entry into Confederation. His had been the most

insistent voice and the most persuasive pen in the long struggle for responsible government, first in the colony and then in
the province, which he served as its second premier. He represented Victoria in the House of Commons for more than a
decade.

He played a distinct, if captious, part in the tangled web of
Canadian railway politics. He fought those who favoured an-
nexation by the United States and, while American interests
were diverted by the Civil War, he advocated the purchase of
Alaska from the Russians in a move that would have changed
the geopolitics of North America. He foresaw Britain and
Canada joined together in a Commonwealth. He argued that
Canadian governors general should be Canadians.

He was one of the first of a still unending line of critics
calling for the abolition, or at least, the restructuring, of the
Senate, and he tried, clumsily, to modernize the divorce laws.
It was a packed and productive, combative and contentious
public life. Yet when his will was probated, his occupation
was simply listed as "retired journalist, etc," and the last
memories that many of his contemporaries had of him were
of the derangement of his final, sad years.

Today he is remembered for the part he played in the
creation of the province of British Columbia, for taking the
province into Confederation and for becoming (in George
Woodcock's words) the man most responsible for the fact
that Canada "eventually did stretch from ocean even unto
ocean."[2] What we remember of the man himself, however, is
often blurred. More precisely, De Cosmos remains an enigma.
While his political life can be traced in some detail, almost

nothing is known of the personality behind the public performance. On his relations with his family, his bachelorhood, his social, sexual, literary and sporting interests, the record is silent. No personal papers exist and the newspapers, notes, diaries and other preserved papers of the time reveal nothing of his private hours. Access to the inner man is blocked. As the historian Robert Kendrick put it, "the vital core of his personality continues to elude us."[3]

The course of De Cosmos' early years in Nova Scotia can be followed in vague outline. After that, from a short note his brother penned in later life, we are able to trace the route he followed when he crossed the continent to the American west, and we are given a hint of his California years. But these are no more than signposts along the way. The moving figure appears only in outline. When he enters political life in British Columbia he comes into sharper focus, as his actions are a matter of public record. There remains little, however, to tell us what manner of man lay behind these actions, and today's writers often settle for saying simply that he was eccentric.

What spurred this Halifax warehouse clerk to set off for the goldfields of California and, almost immediately on arrival there, petition the state's lawmakers to change his name from William Alexander Smith to Amor De Cosmos? And how did he acquire the vocabulary, the professional skill and the wealth of literary allusion to become an instantly successful newspaper editor and — when he was on form — an indefatigable political actor and a fearless dissenter? And what drove him, in the end, insane?

⁂

I had long been intrigued by the elusiveness of the man, and some years ago set out to find answers to some of these questions. I visited Windsor, Nova Scotia, where he was born, Halifax, where he spent his early breadwinning years, as well as Sacramento, Placerville, Oroville and El Dorado, California, where he went in search of a new life and a fortune. I spent time in the Public Archives of British Columbia and the City of Victoria Archives, the Hudson's Bay Company Archives in Winnipeg and the National Public Archives in Ottawa, and I read what others had written about him. The result was that, fascinating as the material is, there was little on which an authentic "life" could be built.

Out of frustration with the lack of detail grew the idea of using what I had seen and read to look behind the major events in his life in order to see if, in this way, I could uncover more of his personality. In the words of the first provincial archivist, quoted in the epigraph on the opening page, another comment had caught my attention. "Facts, statistics, official documents — in fact the entire category of archivist lore — can only in themselves convey an imperfect impression of what they relate to."

What follows then is a possible interpretation of how he came to change his name as well as a study of his life as businessman, journalist and politician, the aim of both being to reach a closer understanding of why historians and others have described him as an enigma.

And the place to start is Nova Scotia.

CHAPTER 1

Halifax

Facts about the lives of the forbears of William Alexander Smith are as scarce as those of his own. Like him, they were dissenters by nature and belief and served on Cromwell's side in the English Civil War. By way of reward, one strand of the family was granted land in Ireland. It was not the most congenial place for new arrivals of the Protestant faith, and, soon after, they decided to emigrate. They made their way via Newfoundland to Nova Scotia, where they settled on farmland in what was eventually Hants County. Although there were early deaths in the family of Jesse and Charlotte Esther Smith, some of those who survived inherited the long-life gene. One daughter lived to a hundred years of age. William's older brother, Charles, who figures significantly in this story, reached eighty-eight years after a series of arduous outdoor careers. And, with the pressure he was under through much of his adult life, William's own seventy-one years was no mean feat.

During his early manhood years in Nova Scotia, four critical elements took both shape and permanence in Smith's young mind: the power of the spoken as well as the written word; the importance of possessing a skill; the consciousness of a larger world of life and letters beyond that of his hometown; and a sharp awareness of the iniquity of uncontrolled power.

Smith was born in August 1825 in Windsor, a town with a population in excess of two thousand that thrived on shipbuilding and the gypsum trade. It was also the site of King's Academy, a distinguished educational foundation, which William attended until, at age fifteen, he moved with his family to Halifax. There, earning his keep became the first call on his time, and further education followed, although only by way of evening classes, membership in the Mechanics Institute and, when he was older, through active participation in the Dalhousie Debating Society.

For a man who brought such extravagant deliberateness to his later life, spending eight years working as a clerk in the wholesale grocery business may seem an unlikely apprenticeship. The firm of William and Charles Witham, however, was an established institution in Halifax. It had been in existence from the beginning of the century and, in the social perceptions of the time, employment in a well-reputed wholesale business carried with it a cachet considerably more acceptable than that of a clerkship in the retail trade of today. It also left young William free, not only to engage in activities that were a substitute for the university education he might have had, but also to master a craft that would become a key part of the longer-term plans that were taking shape in his mind.

In the lives of those with whom he spent these leisure hours, we find clues as to the way his plans culminated in life-shaping action. To extend his formal education, Smith took evening classes that were being offered by John Sparrow Thompson in his own home. Thompson had emigrated from London in search of an environment in which to develop what he believed to be his talent for writing. His son was to become a judge, a politician, and eventually the premier of Nova Scotia.

Thompson was a man of radical views who encouraged young Smith to see that he needed more than a general education if he was to fulfill the ambition that was beginning to engage him. He offered a program which included English literature and "the use of the globes." Mathematics, astronomy and shorthand were added later. Thompson was for many years secretary of the Mechanics Institute and had two spells as editor of the *Novascotian*, the province's most influential newspaper. He thus became Smith's mentor on many counts.

With the idea of adding a craft to his qualifications, Smith approached William Valentine, who had an established photography business in the town. Valentine was no ordinary photographer. He was one of the first in Halifax to use the newly invented process of Jacques Mandé Daguerre, and he was the very first to offer lessons in the new process. Smith saw this as an opportunity to acquire a skill that would serve him well, and when he left for California in 1852, the contents of his kit included a camera and a supply of daguerreotype stock.[1]

Yet well before this occurred, Smith came under a second formative influence in the figure of Joseph Howe. A Nova Scotia journalist, famed for his powers in both the written and the spoken word, Howe had come to the fore when he used a six-hour address to a jury to defend himself against the charge of seditious libel. With this achievement behind him, he entered politics, eventually becoming premier of his province, a member of the House of Commons and, through it all, a battler for responsible government. By the time Smith had reached his majority, Joseph Howe had long been a political presence in the province and, under the tutelage of liberal-reformist friends in the Dalhousie Debating Society, the young Smith became an admirer, looking to emulate Howe's ability to produce the withering comment and colourful insult when moved to anger.

What remained most important for Smith was Howe's struggle for responsible government in Nova Scotia. A principal object of Howe's hostility on this front was Lucius Bentinck Cary, the tenth Viscount Falkland, who had arrived in Halifax in the same year as the Smith family, and served as lieutenant-governor of Nova Scotia from 1840 to 1846. The reason for Howe's loathing was the way in which Cary placed obstacles to the timetable that had been set to introduce responsible government in Nova Scotia.

De Cosmos' own long, tenacious fight for responsible government owed much to his recollection of Falkland's perfidy, as he saw it, and reinforced his deep suspicion and disapproval of the negative role a succession of governors was to play in the battle for responsible government on the West Coast. Howe's detestation was provoked, in part, by Falkland's actions over the payment of officials on the civil list as well as the lieutenant-governor's penchant for communicating secretly with Westminster, issues that later spurred De Cosmos' own assaults on executive power. When, much later, De Cosmos was ultimately elected to the House of Commons, it pleased him enormously that it was Howe and Charles Tupper, another Nova Scotia premier and the sixth prime minister of Canada, who introduced him as a new member of the House.

The question then arises as to why Smith, having secure employment, creative leisure and agreeable guides and mentors, decided to leave for California, and why do so when the gold rush was already three years old? It was not unusual for talented young men to seek fortune and freedom in other and more magnetic fields. Halifax, however, was a city of infinite promise. It had incorporated in 1851. Cunard steamships kept it only fourteen days away from Liverpool and the hub of empire. The social and literary scene was lively enough for Charles Dickens to include it on his North American tour. And new amenities were fast reducing the discomforts of daily life. Gaslight was bringing a brighter glow to office, meeting room and parlour.

The immediate reason for his decision to leave home was

Viscount Falkland, c. 1845. [NSPA]

the home itself. On Lockman Street, Halifax, where the Smiths had their family home, the tenth child had been born in 1845 and, by the time she was five, family life had become crowded and tense. Three sisters, all younger than William, claimed the most attention and, for a man in the full flush of manhood, the cross-currents of the domestic scene caused strain and frustration. Consequently, the idea of going to live and prosper in an environment even more promising than that of Nova Scotia gradually took hold of him.

Smith was slow to put his plan into effect as he was obliged to save enough from his clerk's salary to make the long and

Joseph Howe, 1834. [NSPA]

expensive journey, and to keep him solvent until he could start earning again. This could be achieved only by living at home until he felt financially secure. He was also in no great hurry because, while California had become his chosen destination, he was not planning to join the early mad rush of migrants whose main motive was instant wealth. Moiling for gold was no part of the evolving plan. It was the camera, not the shovel or the pan, that was to assure him of a new source of income.

There was another reason why he was slow to put his plan into action, and it looked suspiciously like nervous procrastination. Even after he had made the decision to leave, he was still trying to judge the most propitious moment. As a regular reader of the *Novascotian*, Smith paid close attention to anything in its columns that had a bearing on his plans. For a number of years the newspaper had been filled with contradictory news about the goldfields. On June 4, 1849, for example, it was expressing caution about life in California. "[T]o intending emigrants we would say, do not be persuaded by others — and do not take a leap in the dark — sit down calmly and count the cost." There would be hardships and privations, it warned, adding, with gentle disparagement, that there was also "the questionable character of which California society must necessarily be composed."

At about the same time, however, separate accounts from the field were beginning to be more positive. Californian gold arriving in Philadelphia had been valued at nearly three and a half million dollars, enough to encourage any restless spirit to make up his bedding roll. Then, two weeks later, Smith read

"...alas, what a host of these adventurers are numbered among the dead." Next he would find the paper celebrating an old Halifax knife grinder who had travelled overland to the West, "wheeling before him his apparatus." How much simpler, then, would it be for an able-bodied younger man to pack his daguerreotype equipment and head for the Overland Trail?

Then, in December 1850, cholera was reported on the trail. In no time at all, though, cholera had "disappeared." There was exciting news from the "New Diggings," followed by a discouraging report that a large number of miners had been forced to spend the winter in Salt Lake City. It was bewildering counsel.

And there was yet another reason for his hesitation. The Californian mining camp that grew most rapidly after the discovery of gold at Sutter's Mill was Dry Diggin, named after the way miners moved cartloads of dry soil to running water to separate the gold from the soil. Its growth made it the natural place for a young entrepreneur to choose as his journey's end. Well before Smith had planned to set out, however, Dry Diggin had become a settlement with a widespread reputation for violent behaviour and summary justice. It was soon known as Hangtown — reason enough for De Cosmos to have second thoughts.

Two events then came together to stiffen his resolve. The first was a report that California had amended its criminal code to require a more rigorous jury selection in those parts of the state such as Hangtown, where impromptu citizens' juries administered what was known as lynch law or vigilante justice. The prospect of a more settled community seemed to be in prospect and, indeed, in 1854, Hangtown was renamed Placerville. It was soon to become the third largest town in California.

The second timely event occurred in September 1851 when the *Novascotian* declared that the reports from all the mining districts were more favourable than at any period during the previous year. With this account, Smith had acquired all the assurances he needed and was ready to leave.

CHAPTER 2

Westward

There were three ways for Smith to travel to the goldfields of California. First was the voyage around the Horn, which was the longest distance but the shortest in time. Or one could sail to the Isthmus of Panama and, after 1855, cross on the railway and then sail up the West Coast to California. The third route was the overland route, certainly the most arduous but also the least expensive. This is what Smith chose. About his journey westward there is little on record except for what his brother Charles recorded in a summary many years later, in 1910. The account begins as follows:

> On leaving his home in Halifax [Smith] went to New York
> and from there crossed the continent to St. Louis on the

Missouri River, at that time on the very outskirts of civil[iz]-
ation. There he joined a party who were leaving for California, but on account of indian [sic] troubles and other obstruc-
tions on the way they were obliged to remain at Salt Lake for
the winter as they were too late to cross the Sierra Nevada
mountains.[1]

Any search for the "vital core" of De Cosmos' personality
must account for his time on this long journey to California.
Unfortunately, his brother's account is of limited value, partly
because it was written fifty years after the events it describes,
and partly because it is difficult to see how its source could
have been other than Smith's own remote, fallible and probably embellished recollection. In any case, it is not enough in
itself on which to base any serious findings or reflections on
the part the journey played in the development of his character and career. There has to be more.

From other sources one can conclude that on reaching the
Missouri River, he made his way to St. Joseph, one of the
staging posts from which the Overland Trail began. Here he
joined a group of about forty in number, composed of gold
seekers and others who were assembling the equipment and
provisions needed for the journey. This company, as it was
called, either appointed a captain or engaged a guide whose
responsibility it would be to keep the wagon train on course,
establish routines, select sites for the nightly stopover and
resolve any differences that might arise among what was in-
evitably a highly disparate group.

For the first time in his life, Smith was to find himself
spending weeks living, day and night, among strangers, some

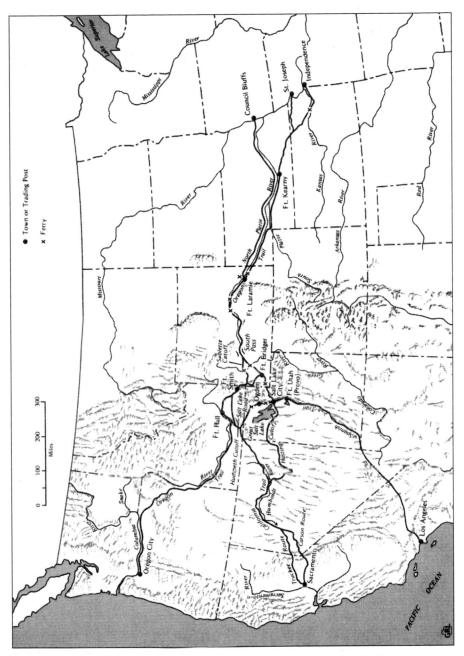

Map of the Overland Trail during the California Gold Rush.

of whose beliefs and attitudes were vastly different from the traditional code he had been taught to observe. It acted as a short, intensive and provoking course in human relations. It made a lasting impression on him.

Smith's brother had spoken of what he called "indian troubles." One of the many stories about Smith that enjoyed a long run in Victoria told of the critical part he played in fighting off an attack on his wagon train. It is impossible to confirm the story, but against this tale of heroic action must be set the fact that he was making the journey three years after the gold find at Sutter's Mill had triggered the trek of the forty-niners. The steady traffic of men, covered wagons and animals, and the accumulated knowledge of the terrain and its dangers meant that, by 1852, the first nine hundred miles of the trail had become well marked and more secure. Moreover, the majority of travellers on this leg were now families heading for Oregon and those parts of California where they hoped to find fertile virgin land on which to settle and farm.

Thus an "indian" raid was, in these circumstances, an unlikely occurrence. The more likely cause of any disruptive delay was an accident or a breakdown in equipment. In fact, from what can be inferred, this was the fate of Smith's company. The delay in repairing the damage was so long that they realized it would be impossible for them to reach the Sierra Mountains before winter snows had blocked the passes. They had no alternative but to make for Salt Lake City and spend the winter there.

The speed at which a covered-wagon train moved was determined by its size and the strength and number of the horses or oxen that drew it. Diaries of the time show that on a good day a company would cover no more than fifteen to eighteen miles. Even without delays, it would take eight to ten weeks to reach Salt Lake City and the routine would not vary:

> For nine hundred miles west of the Missouri River, every day was like the last. Rise before dawn, cook and eat breakfast, gather the animals, hitch up the wagons, head out, halt around midday, cook and eat dinner, march again to whatever camp the captain or scouts had discovered, then once again cook and eat supper, set guards on the stock and go to sleep under the stars or the canvas.[2]

For Smith and others of his temperament, it meant that boredom was high on the list of possible perils. Back in Halifax, Smith had shown himself to be of a measured and cautious disposition. On this stretch of the trail, annoyance at the setback, the slow speed of travel, the often irksome fellowship and a sense that his plans were coming apart caused signs of an impatient streak in his character to surface.

For the time being, his agitation was deflected by a new interest: the world of the Mormons.[3] To cross rivers, companies were obliged to use ferries that were invariably manned by Mormons. The only inhabitants in this newly settled land with the equipment and skill to fix broken axles or twisted wheels on damaged wagons were Mormons. And they were ready traders; if companies found that they had bought the wrong kind of vehicle for the terrain, enterprising Mormons could be found who would offer a lighter wagon in exchange for, say, two of the heavier make.

Moreover, a winter in Salt Lake City meant negotiating with the settlers for the accommodation they needed for themselves and their equipment. It was with Mormons that they conducted the normal transactions of daily living. If they arrived ill from the effects of the journey, they benefitted from whatever medication and care the Mormons could provide. The contacts were many and varied but it was not all sweetness and light. In the frustrations of an involuntary stay, disputes over beliefs and behaviour were frequent. The effect on Smith, with his commitment to self-improvement and increased knowledge, led him to spend much of his time in the study of Mormon beliefs and practices.

It was almost inevitable that any trekker who had spent a winter in Salt Lake City would later find that some vague tale, flattering or incriminating or both, had been woven around his existence there. It was a fate from which a man who changed his name would certainly not be exempt. In De Cosmos' case, it gave rise to a scurrilous *canard* of late Victorian origin that he had made off with precious Mormon memorabilia, and that this was the real reason for his strange behaviour on arrival in California.

Still more unbelievable was the story that he was tempted to consider a more permanent stay, but was forced to make a getaway when Brigham Young, the President of the Church of Latter Day Saints and founder of Salt Lake City, tried to make him marry and settle there. It was a fable that followed him. "Mormon Bill" was a favourite taunt of hecklers at his public meetings in Victoria.

Salt Lake City, with a population of over eight thousand at

this time, had at least one flourishing photography business, and it was to be expected that Smith should visit it and show his professional interest. Again the event was distorted. In a biographical dictionary of professional photographers of the period, it is alleged that he became a partner in a firm of photographers in Salt Lake City and that he planned to return there after a stay in California. The photograph of him in the dictionary is authentic but the biographical details accompanying it are so totally inaccurate as to make it plain that a profusion of Smiths had confused the compilers.[4]

While most of the stories about Smith in Salt Lake City are clearly fabrications, there is enough of a common theme to suggest that he gave some thought to the idea of starting a new life among a different, rule-abiding and purposeful population. In spite of the extra cost of an extended stay in Salt Lake City, solvency seems never to have been a problem for him, and it is obvious that he became more than an anonymous presence during his winter stay in the city.

In addition, he learnt from his daily observations of the Mormon community at work, at play and at worship, that the successful pursuit of a new way of living required a clear sense of purpose and an applied resourcefulness. By the time he had reached the end of the trail, it will be clear that he had put his own unique interpretation on these basic precepts.

With the onset of spring, Smith and his company began to re-equip themselves and their reconstituted wagon train in readiness for what was to be the most gruelling leg of the journey. It was not only more rugged and dangerous than the first sector, but the nature of the terrain made it impossible to establish a reliable, well-marked trail. They were now to set out to cross the Great Salt Lake Desert, reputed to be the most forbidding desert on the continent.

Here it is that we first see that impetuosity in Smith that was later to become so evident. After only a short while with the company, he decided that they were too slow and he set off on his own. Charles recalled his brother's experiences after Smith and his company had left the City of the Saints:

> ...after some four or five days of slow travelling along the trail, he decided to go on alone, as he had a good horse and could travel much faster than the party he was with. Having provided himself with plenty of food and ammunition for his rifle and pistol, he left the train and by fast travelling soon reached the Humboldt Valley and followed the river until he came to the crossing, then following the trail until he came to where it branched off into Northern California. When he reached that point he and his horse were suffering terribly from drinking alkali water, as he was not able to find any other, however, he pushed on as rapidly as possible and soon found fresh water which revived him and his [horse] and in a few days he arrived in Placerville, California, in June 1853.[5]

The earliest migrants on the California trails knew that, for the first three days out from Salt Lake City, there would be no drinking water within reach, and they feared, from all the stories they had heard, that, along the rest of the route, the prospects might never be any better.[6] The agony of a long searing thirst in a hot, dry climate induced a frenzy in which trekkers would drink the first water they came across. If, in their confused state, they found that it had the taste of lye, they knew they had swallowed water with an alkali concentrate so high that it was debilitating and disorienting to men and often deadly to beasts.

What becomes apparent from his brother's account is that Smith, travelling alone, drank from a poisoned source, and he "suffered terribly," losing his direction either in the Humboldt Sink, a wide, white alkali expanse over which a fine, blinding dust drifted, or on the belt of desert beyond.

The Humboldt, a contemporary diarist said, "is not good for man nor beast . . . and there is not timber in three hundred miles of its desolate valley to make a snuff box, or sufficient vegetation along its banks to shade a rabbit, while its waters contain the alkali to make soap for a nation."[7] His brother's account downplays the event. It gives the impression that this young man who, having been so incredibly foolhardy as to follow this route alone and endure what was, in effect, a near-death experience, regained his strength and self-assurance, negotiated the difficult and dangerous crossing of the Sierra Nevada Mountains and then calmly cantered on to the last sector of the Carson Trail and into Placerville.

It is an inadequate account, as subsequent developments confirm. What seems equally unbelievable but apparently true is that, three weeks after his arrival in Placerville, the wagon train he had deserted arrived with his photographic equipment intact.[8]

CHAPTER 3

The Transformation

There are many reasons people invoke for wanting to change their name. Often it is to signal a clear separation from their kin. They dislike the name they were born with — or married into. They hate the sound of it or the look of it on paper. The name might be just painfully commonplace, or it does not describe the kind of person they believe themselves to be. It causes them to be mistaken for someone else. They need to hide from the fame or infamy attached to it. And so on.

Smith may have been impetuous but he was a law-abiding young man. There is no known foundation to the rumours that the reason for a speedy name change was that he had committed a crime in Salt Lake City or that he had joined one of the many self-appointed local community groups who were taking the law into their own hands. Another rumour sprang from the time he spent in Mud Springs, which was not only the centre of a mining district but a flourishing cross-roads for freight and stage lines. It had derived its sombre name from the boggy quagmire that cattle and horses had made of a nearby watering place. Civic pride eventually took hold and it too sought an exotic name change. It became El Dorado. This, it was alleged, had inspired Smith to make his own grandiloquent gesture. In fact, a plaque in the main street reminds visitors that Mud Springs was incorporated as El Dorado in April 1855, more than a year after Smith's own transformation.

It was customary for the *Placerville Herald* to print a letter list advising homesick miners that there was mail for them. In the month Smith arrived in Placerville, the list included twenty-four Smiths. It also appears that there was a William Alexander Smith living in San Francisco who had changed his name because there were others with the same given names. Even so, the theory that this was the real reason for the name change does not stand up to reasonable scrutiny. It is obvious that he could have received his mail with a less exotic identity than the one he chose — Amor De Cosmos.

The idea for the change of name had its origin long before he reached Placerville. He had spent many hours on that eventful ride, reflecting on his past, pondering the nature of his ambition, imagining the kind of life he hoped to enjoy in the newer world. He asked himself if a reformulation of his own attitudes and beliefs, even a deliberate and controlled reconstruction of his existing personality, would help him to confront and profit from the new challenges he was about to face. Did it lie in his power to cease being what he was and to transform himself into a quite different being? This was not an absurd possibility. After all, had not David Hume, whose philosophy had so often been the topic at the Dalhousie Debating Society, questioned the unchanging continuity of our perceptions of who we were, and asked if we could be certain that we were always the same person and not a multiple personality?

The atmosphere of Salt Lake City, spiritually strange and disconcerting, had freed him from old assumptions. It allowed his disordered musings to consider new and extravagant scenarios. Then, after he had taken the reckless step of galloping out on his own, he endured that thirst-driven chase that led to physical pain, mental disorder and a temporary loss in his sense of direction. It was well-known that suicides on this sector of the trek were not uncommon. In one day on the Humboldt, three men and two women had tried to drown themselves and, after well-wishers pulled them from the water, they immediately threw themselves back in, so intent were they on escaping the daily horror.[1] "He who arrived in California," wrote another chronicler of the trail, "was a different person from the one who had started from the east. Experience in so short a time fused his elements into something new."[2]

The effect of this episode on Smith was life changing. It was in the hours, stretching into the days and weeks that it took him to reach Placerville, that the idea of recreating himself became urgent and irresistible. He had had a near-death experience, and he now felt free to prescribe and assume a new persona, one that would set him apart from other men and give him licence and authority. His experience with the abundance of Smiths in Placerville may have encouraged him to speed up his plan but, whatever the immediate impulse, within six months he had established himself as a resident of both Placerville and Mud Springs in El Dorado county. This meant that he could engage the services of the lawyer and senator, Gaven D. Hall, to steer a bill through the California legislature that officially changed the name of this young stranger from William Alexander Smith to Amor De Cosmos.

Much has been made of the heavy jocularity with which the legislators in Sacramento debated the proposal. Would not Amor Muggins De Cosmos be more American? If not, why not go all the way in arrogance and self-advertisement and become Amor De Cosmos Caesar? And so on. The noble senators and assemblymen passed the bill, but not without one final complaint: that the "De" was pretentious and "furrin," to which the petitioner replied, "I desire not to adopt the name of Amor De Cosmos because it smacks of a foreign title but because it is an unusual name and its meaning tells what I love most: love of order, beauty, the world, the universe."[3]

If the swagger in this explanation did not alert the honourable members to the possibility that they had performed a legislative service for a crank, the more learned among them would have noted the mix of affectation and erudition in the three parts of a name with a combined Latin, French or Spanish, and Greek derivation. They might have observed that

Original draft of an act
to change the name of
William Alexander Smith
to Amor De Cosmos.
[CALIFORNIA STATE
ARCHIVES]

39

this incongruity showed that much passion but little serious consideration had gone into choosing them. This was not the construct of a trained mind but of a lively autodidact and a bright member of the Dalhousie Debating Society. What is more disconcerting is that the act and the wording were the first identifiable sign of an arrogance that, like his impatience and impetuosity, was to grow with time.

It may have been a flagrant display of self-esteem, dramatically and humourlessly enacted, but he was crystal clear as to its purpose. It would separate him from his past and from old relationships, and steel him to face new ones. And this is where the trouble began. A severe mental control was required for it to be successful. The transformed self would also require the possession of a severely restrained manner. The new persona could not show any sign of faltering, of slipping back into its old self. His natural feelings would need to be kept in check, contained and reshaped, if he was to acquire and demonstrate the new self-assurance and achieve the success he was prescribing for himself. The question was: Could he pull it off? The rest of his life is, in effect, the story of how and if he managed it, and at what cost. The price, it turned out, was his sanity.

Before leaving the subject of his name change, there is another possible source of Smith's decision in Sacramento to change it, and in this case, it gives a hint of his later decision to publish a newspaper. This involved the account that reached him, on his California travels, of the career of James King, who, tired of being one of the innumerable James Kings living in Virginia, changed his name to "James King of

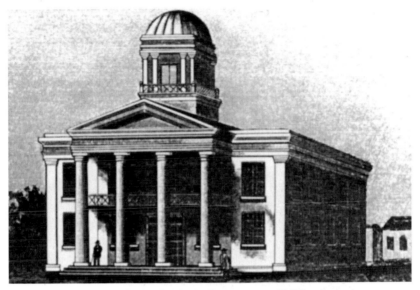

The old courthouse in Sacramento, California.
[CALIFORNIA STATE LIBRARY]

William." When, because of poor health, he decided to move to a better climate, he took his title with him. He first thought to settle in Valparaiso, but then news of the gold finds in California reached him, and King made his way to San Francisco, arriving in November 1848. He then journeyed on to the Sierra goldfields (some say actually to Placerville) and spent a brief and profitable time in the mining business.

King's poor health, however, made the life there physically unbearable and he returned to San Francisco. Having had some experience of the banking business in Virginia, he opened a private banking house, which soon went broke through unwise investments and dishonest colleagues. This forced him to become the salaried employee of another bank,

James King of William, 1856.

which also failed. Two failures coming one after the other led a suspicious public to gossip about his own part in them.

In order to rebut any charges of shady dealing, King produced a steady flow of pamphlets and newspaper articles in his own defence. The experience gave him a yearning to have a newspaper of his own, and he proceeded to produce the very successful *Daily Evening Bulletin*. He then wrote and published a series of well-documented accounts detailing what he personally knew of the forms of extortion, debt repudiation and other kinds of criminal activity and political jiggery-pokery that could be traced to firms and individuals in San Francisco. He soon acquired a reputation as a crusader against corruption in the city. This made him subject to threats and, in May 1856, a man who had been the target of his most serious accusations shot him in the street. He died some days later. A vast crowd attended his funeral. "With a bold pen, he assailed giant evils," wrote one mourner.

Smith had followed closely this story of a newspaperman who had not only changed his name but by so doing had discovered in himself a crusading spirit and the means to express it.

CHAPTER 4

The Transition

In 1853 in California, five years after the first frenetic rush, gold extraction by the early, primitive methods was no longer producing instant wealth. More efficient tools were needed. Soon rocker and sluice boxes and pumps of a more efficient design were becoming essential equipment. At the same time, the formless mining centres began to take shape as established towns, and Placerville, as has been noted, was one of the most important. For De Cosmos, its history of summary, oak tree justice, the new wealth and the still-brooding violence gave it a certain allure. With the choice of a dozen hotels (the Placer, the Iowa, the Philadelphia, the What Cheer, among the more reputable, and a nourishing diet of the famous local dish, Hangtown Fry), it was a stimulating environment in which to shape and advance his plans, using the one marketable skill at his command.

Setting himself up as professional photographer, however, proved to be difficult, for the ground was already occupied. In February 1854, for example, there was an advertisement in the Placerville newspaper, the *Mountain Democrat*, addressed to "ladies and gentlemen." It stated that, by using the daguerreotype method, a John Salmon was available to take photographs that "cannot be excelled by any other establishment of the state." Shortly after, De Cosmos attempted to establish a similar project in Sacramento, but this came to naught; here, too, there was competition.

Soon he realized that he needed to look elsewhere for his clientele if he was to make a living with the camera. He decided that, even though activity at the diggings had passed its peak, a promising prospect lay with the miner who would pay to have his picture taken on his own plot. It could serve as tangible proof that he had staked out his claim. It would help to warn off the unprincipled adventurer. It would also provide him with a way to convey evidence and assurance to the "folks back home."

The original Daguerre process required a large quantity of both equipment and time. The Petzval lens, however, which had appeared in 1840, and which Valentine had acquired in Halifax, made it possible to lighten the load and to shorten the time required for the picture to develop. It also allowed a town photographer to charge as little as two dollars a shot. With a pan, pick and shovel costing fifty dollars or more in local stores, it was not unreasonable for De Cosmos to charge twenty dollars for a session on location. And it was a business that flourished by word of mouth. For a time he found it to be lucrative but, as with most things in boom towns, it would not last.

An aspect of the photography business to which little attention was paid at the time was the damage the frequent use the chemicals — mercury, vapours of iodine, bromine, chlorine and so on — could cause to the nervous system through inhalation and ingestion. Whether or not this played a part in the deteriorating state of De Cosmos' last years, it was an occupational hazard of the time.[1]

Back in Placerville, just as the new life, the new direction and the new persona were all taking shape, another physical presence, while not unwelcome in itself, threatened to upset the entire, carefully conceived project. It would test him with reminders of his former life. It would also provide him with a vital ally.

Charles McKeivers Smith, William's older brother by three years, was a natural handyman, a born entrepreneur, and more of a natural adventurer than his brother. He left school at twelve and worked on a farm until he was fifteen. Local records show him earning pocket money tidying the cemetery and mending fences. He left home at fifteen to learn the trade of carriage building and the making of farm implements. At seventeen he moved to Halifax and engaged in house building and what, in later recollections, he called "trading on the coast," a term that could cover many an exotic enterprise in Nova Scotia's bays and inlets. When a boundary dispute flared up between Maine and New Brunswick, he volunteered to serve in his country's militia.

On January 2, 1854, two years after William had left Halifax, Charles took passage on the *Britannia*, a Cunarder bound for Boston. There he transferred to a vessel sailing to Aspinwall, Panama, where he crossed the Isthmus, and boarded a ship to San Francisco. It is not known if there had been any communication between the brothers in the intervening two years. Charles certainly showed no great urge to see his brother, staying in San Francisco for three months, exploring the endless and enticing opportunities the city offered a man of his abilities.

If he had not heard previously of brother William's exotic name change, it would almost certainly have been known among the contacts he was making in the city. Eventually he decided to visit Placerville to learn the mystery behind his brother's strange alias.

The meeting of the two men in a foreign environment, one reflective, cerebral and odd, the other, down-to-earth, footloose and practical, might have led nowhere. As it was, both were shrewd enough to see in the exciting prospects around them the possibility of a fruitful collaboration, and decided to act on it.

With the decline in gold extraction and, with it, the photography business, De Cosmos had been looking for some other way of both building up his capital and reigniting his sense of adventure. Given the environment in which he was living, it was not altogether surprising that he should have found it in land speculation. He was also persuaded that it was a skill for which he had a natural affinity. In no time at all, the brothers were to be seen working in tandem, scouting out the country from the Yuba River in the north down to the Mexican border, acquiring property and mineral rights, photographing mining claims (their own as well as others) and doing what Charles described as "business of other kinds."

By the end of his third year in the country, De Cosmos was not only a well-known figure in the region but was giving some consideration to the idea of establishing himself in this part of California. It was the spur that led him to buy a property in Oroville in Butte County and to join Oroville Lodge, Number 103, of the Masonic Order.[2]

Successful as he was, however, it was becoming clear to him that it would be a long time before he acquired the considerable capital he needed to establish a position of indisputable influence and, with it, the power base he had envisaged for himself. And, as usual, he was in a hurry. Thus, when news of the Fraser River gold discovery reached Butte County in late April 1858, he sensed that his main chance had come. His tendency to take precipitate action took over. Eighteen thousand seekers after new riches left California in May, June and July 1858, and De Cosmos was one of the first. He went immediately to San Francisco, took passage on board the *Brother Jonathan*, and, by the sixteenth of May, was in Victoria, ready to make a quick reconnaissance.

What he found met all his expectations. He saw a replay of the Californian scene as he had first encountered it. This time, however, the prospect rose before him of fulfilling more completely the destiny he had foreseen immediately after those frightening days on the Humboldt trail. Now it could be achieved in a British colony. He returned immediately to Oroville and persuaded his brother that there were rich pickings for a man of his diverse and imaginative talents. The tax records of Oroville County show two notations in the name of De Cosmos, the second covering the sale of the Oroville property immediately before he left for Vancouver Island.[3] He was back in Victoria by the end of June.

Charles, who followed his brother, quickly presented himself in Victoria as an architect and builder. He planned and assisted in the erection of a number of government buildings. He spent time as a gold digger in the Cariboo. A group of merchants in Victoria's Wharf Street, hearing of a copper find in the Queen Charlotte Islands, commissioned him to check

Street in Oroville, California, where De Cosmos lived before moving to Victoria, B.C., c. 1856. [OROVILLE PIONEER HISTORY MUSEUM]

on its extent. He was one of the first prospectors on the limited Leech River gold find on southern Vancouver Island and, a year later, was prospecting for ore on the shores of Kootenay Lake. Back in Victoria, he set up a fish-canning business. Later, when De Cosmos entered federal politics and was obliged to spend more time in Ottawa, Charles took charge of the *Victoria Daily Standard*, his brother's second newspaper.

Charles was fifty before he married. His wife died within a year of their marriage after giving birth to a son. Resourceful as his life showed him to be, he was, by all accounts, a reticent and retiring man. In the outline he gives of his brother's life in California, he makes no mention of himself. He is able to describe De Cosmos' photographic and speculative activities because he accompanied him on many of his forays, a fact he also fails to mention.[4] He writes of his brother's decision to leave California for Victoria without saying that he followed him. He records that his brother "returned to California, settled up his business there and came back to Victoria...in which place he made his home up to the time of his death."[5] Again, there is no mention of his own presence. De Cosmos was not the only member of the Smith family to have an elusive element in his make-up.

In De Cosmos' last months, Charles was attentive and protective and was the executor of his brother's will. He died in 1911 and was mourned as one of the noted pioneers of the city.

CHAPTER 5

Victoria:
Business Strategies

In 1858 Governor Douglas issued an edict to the effect that gold seekers from the south planning to join the Fraser Canyon gold rush had to travel via Victoria to obtain a miner's licence. Soon after his arrival in Victoria, however, De Cosmos heard stories of a throng defying Douglas and following a land trail to the goldfields. He once told an audience that, on his arrival in Victoria, he saw that what the city needed was an honest newspaper but that he had initially planned to enter the fishing and lumbering business. With all this activity on the mainland, it occurred to him that he might find there a more promising opportunity to establish himself, build up his capital and construct a power base. He had barely found his land legs before he was taking to the sea again.

A sketch of early Victoria, B.C.

A flow of goods and passengers was already crossing the Juan de Fuca Strait from Victoria to the mainland (in what is now the United States), and the *Leviathan*, a schooner-rigged steam yacht, was one of a number of vessels that came up from San Francisco to Victoria, ready to profit from this trade. On July 24, 1858, the *Leviathan* was about to sail on its first crossing with D. W. Higgins on board.

David William Higgins was born in Halifax but educated in New York. After serving an apprenticeship as a journeyman printer, he made his way to San Francisco where he assisted in the launch of a newspaper. News of the gold rush brought him to Victoria and eventually on to Yale, B.C., where he became a store owner and a speculator in the mining business. He later became a man of substance, a publisher, an editor, an author and Speaker of the B.C. Legislative Assembly.

Higgins was a significant figure in De Cosmos' life as friend, then foe and, much later, admirer. Late in life, Higgins recalled their first encounter, and in it a clear profile emerges of De Cosmos at this period and in his new role. Higgins had just boarded the *Leviathan* when another passenger, carrying a brown overcoat and a travelling bag, joined him:

> I found my fellow passenger a very agreeable companion. He was about 30 years of age and very well informed. He, too, had come from California and had settled at Victoria, which he pronounced the most peaceful spot in the world, surpassing even his own native city of Halifax. He told me his name was Amor De Cosmos, and that he was bound for the American town of Semiahmoo, to examine its possibilities as a commercial rival of Victoria. As I was bound for the same place, we became very communicative and whiled away the tedious passage to Port Townsend by relating our experiences in the Golden State. At Port Townsend the boat remained until morning and we got accommodation at one of the hotels. . . . The next afternoon we reached Semiahmoo. . . . We remained at Semiahmoo several days and then returned by a sailing barque to Victoria, where I parted from my new-found friend.[1]

As both Higgins and De Cosmos were to discover, it would be a stormy friendship.

De Cosmos' assessment of his visit to Port Townsend and the environs was that the area did not have the promise he was looking for, and he sailed back to Victoria, ready to

S.Y. *Leviathan* on which Higgins and De Cosmos first met. It later became Governor Seymour's private yacht, c. 1867. [BCPA A-00087]

embark, among other things, on building up what became an extensive, if tangled, real estate portfolio. Examples of his speculative forays include an application for the right to work a quartz claim on the San Juan River, permission to erect a mill or mills on the Mutchlat River, a request to rent 250 acres on the Indian Reserve in Cowichan and the purchase of land in Comox. He also owned substantial property in the Chinese quarter of Victoria.

While he was premier, he and others were accused of taking advantage of private information about an iron ore discovery on Texada Island, off the east coast of Vancouver Island. An inquiry found them innocent but many were not convinced. As a witness said at the inquiry, "De Cosmos was

David W. Higgins. [BCPA E-01366]

always dabbling in ore." In one of his earliest speeches in the House of Commons, he spoke of men "of the highest attainment" who were engaged in "economic geology," a term that might equally have been the euphemism that neatly defined the unspecified activities that occupied him and his brother during their time together in California and which he continued to pursue.[2] It undoubtedly describes and dignifies the business of dabbling in mining claims.

When he seemed most engrossed in the political process, a weather eye was always cocked for the possibilities of undeveloped space. With the continued exercise of these two skills, his material needs were met for the rest of his life. Shortly before his retirement from politics, a published list of land holdings by residents showed him to be eighth in order of worth. Among the possessions he left behind at his death were four steel safes in which there were records of holdings so numerous, complex and confusing that the Department of Finance was forced to agree to a delay in the probating of his will.

He was a firm, often an outraged, denier of any accusation of business impropriety. In California, his anxiety to avoid the charge of being a newcomer, with fly-by-night intentions, had led him to seek business respectability and reputable connections by becoming a Mason. He wished to have the same cachet and protection in Victoria, and it is relevant to his story to describe the actions he took to this end.

Soon after he had launched the *British Colonist*, an advertisement appeared in the paper calling for a meeting to establish a Masonic Lodge in the town. There is no record of who made the insertion. A meeting was held, a request for its establishment was sent to the Grand Lodge in England and, after protracted discussions, a charter setting up Victoria Lodge, number 1085, arrived on March 20, 1860. It was formally inaugurated in August. The charter members, who were installed by Mr. Robert Burnaby, a Past Master, were a merchant, a solicitor, a draper, a broker, a publican, a carrier, a "gentleman" — and an editor. The membership fee was twelve dollars. De Cosmos was more than a charter member; he was its secretary for the first six months.

His was too volatile a character, however, to spend time and energy on maintaining relationships he found to be of no assistance in his ambitious plans. His active interest faded and, after two years as a member, he arranged to be demitted. Seven years after he had ceased to be a member, he wrote to the secretary of the lodge to complain that "fellow freemasons," John Robson and David Higgins, had contributed to a false rumour in which he was being maligned.[3] The episode is significant in that it illustrates two of De Cosmos' consistent failings, both of which affected much of his political career. One was an inability to overlook any opportunity to protest at a perceived personal affront. The other was an inability to work in harmony with other people for any prolonged period. They were also weaknesses of which he appeared to be either unconscious or unheeding.

CHAPTER 6

The Newspaperman

Newspapers were not a rare feature of life in Victoria in the 1850s. Nor was their production a particularly challenging task. With a moderate amount of journalistic talent, access to a hand press and some assured advertising revenue, the printing and distribution of a new journal presented no serious difficulty. For its size, population and location, Victoria had a high proportion of literate and cultured citizens, so it was comparatively easy to capture a ready, if fickle, readership. Moreover, gold rushes seemed to energize would-be press magnates. The first California newspaper, for example, appeared in 1846, but by 1860 the state was being served by more than a hundred dailies and weeklies.

In Victoria there was a comparable contagion. Ten newspapers were started between 1858 and 1860. Some lasted from two to four years; others took only a few months to disappear. But with flair, fluency, a recognizable target or two and a capacity for righteous indignation, all of which De Cosmos came to possess in abundance, a long street life could be assured.[1]

The *Victoria Gazette*, which had the widest circulation at the time of his arrival in town, had only been in existence for a short time. It had been started by three Americans who had brought their printing press with them from San Francisco. They had planned to call it the *Anglo-American* and, while a sample issue appeared under that banner, they were saved from this gaffe before the first issue hit the streets. By then, its masthead carried *Victoria Gazette* in large letters and, beneath it, *Anglo-American* in smaller type. Soon, the sub-head disappeared altogether and the paper's circulation expanded rapidly. It presented itself as a semi-official gazette commenting innocuously on matters of local interest, expansively on mining developments and sycophantically on the policies of the governor.

Its tone, content and emphasis were anathema to any anti-establishment man, and they played a large part in leading De Cosmos to declare that Victoria needed an honest newspaper. *Le Courier de la Nouvelle Calédonie* also appeared in the first half of 1858 but lasted for only nine issues. De Cosmos swiftly acquired its hand press and the *British Colonist* was born. It would have appealed to his free-thinking spirit to know that the hand press had been donated by the

Society for the Propagation of the Gospels for the use of the first Roman Catholic bishop of Victoria.

The first issue of the *British Colonist* appeared on December 11, 1858, less than six months after De Cosmos' arrival in Victoria. It was composed of four pages. Two hundred copies were printed. The editorial made it immediately and abundantly clear that its tone would be neither passive nor sycophantic. He declared that it was his intention to foster loyalty to the "parent government" and "to determinedly oppose every influence tending to undermine or subvert the existing connection between the colonies and the mother country." In what would now be called a mission statement, he announced his intention "to advocate such changes as will tend to establish self-government" and to "counsel the introduction of responsible government."[2] He also argued for overland communication that would link all the colonies of British North America. The crucial point, however, and one that no one missed was the idea of "self-government" and "responsible government." These were ideas that were anathema to the ruling elite.

Having taken this bold and statesmanlike stance, he then got down to the business of attacking his principal targets with panache and pejoratives. Pre-eminent among them was Governor Douglas himself. James Douglas had been both chief factor of the Hudson's Bay Company and governor of Vancouver Island since 1851. On the creation of British Columbia as a crown colony in 1858, he relinquished his role as chief factor of the Hudson's Bay Company and became the colony's first governor.

In the second issue of the *British Colonist*, De Cosmos lashed out at the insidious role of the Hudson's Bay Company, and accused Douglas and his officials of "toadyism, consanguinity, and incompetency." It was an attack which he sustained long enough for Dr. J. S. Helmcken, the son-in-law of Governor Douglas and Speaker of the House, to find him "hostile, vituperative and abusive to the Governor, the government and everything in general," adding that "it pleased the dissatisfied."[3] It was an opinion shared by the business elite on Victoria's Wharf Street.

There was, however, a growing interest in the reform movement led by De Cosmos, especially by those like John Muir, one of the earliest settlers who had purchased property at Sooke for a farm and sawmill, and who wanted more representative government to meet the needs of those not affiliated to the Hudson's Bay Company.[4] The main difficulty as De Cosmos saw it was that all power worked downwards through patronage from Douglas. As Margaret Ross has noted, De Cosmos went after "the unhealthy influence of the Governor in every branch of government, executive, legislative and judicial."[5]

De Cosmos pointed out that even from the time of the first assembly in 1856, Douglas and his friend John Work had made patronage appointments. De Cosmos was particularly incensed by their actions in connection with the representation of Nanaimo in the assembly and it presaged the trickery with which he would be confronted in Victoria when his time came to stand for election. Douglas had appointed John Frederick Kennedy as a member for Nanaimo, alleging that a grant from the Hudson's Bay Company allowed this. Then in May 1859, De Cosmos warned of the same high-handed activity when Kennedy died and there was a new election. George Barnston of Victoria was nominated by a Captain Stuart, the only elector. The seconder was an assistant in the Hudson's Bay Company store at Nanaimo, who was himself a non-elector. In the event, Barnston never even took his seat.

Spurred on by De Cosmos' attacks, a new election was called, and a captain of a Hudson's Bay Company ship was elected, while he was absent, and elected by one vote. De Cosmos wrote that he was elected "not to represent the people of Nanaimo; but to misrepresent them, to render the country superlatively ridiculous. The historian will write the farce down as the constitution of one, the majority of one, the representation of one, and that the election of one was won by Governor Douglas' able administration."[6]

A famous issue of the *British Colonist*, that of April 2, 1859, contained an article which did more than call for the removal of Douglas and his government, "with its lick-spittle characteristics, its crawling and evil proclivities, its thousand and one faces, and all the corruption which it has engendered." It demanded that the British authorities "curb its profligate extravagance.... They must show it to the world in its hideousness of sin, that honesty may blush and bow the head." Neither the article nor the issue saw the light of day.

By coincidence or through leaked intelligence, the governor's aides reached back at that moment to invoke statutes passed in the reigns of George II and III, which required newspapers to post bonds and sureties in the amount of £800

The *Colonist* building on Government Street after it
moved from Wharf Street. [BCPA A-07820]

to ensure payment of fines or civil damages in the event of a conviction for libel. De Cosmos immediately let it be understood that he did not possess the sum required, and the edition of April 2 did not appear.

It was a sign of the support, or at least the lively interest the views of the paper had gained in certain sections of his readership, that a public meeting was immediately called and donations readily raised to meet the sum needed. At the same time, De Cosmos took the opportunity to condemn the action as an infringement of the constitutional rights of the colonists. The *British Colonist* reappeared on the streets of Victoria but, with that carefully hidden talent for caution that he could occasionally muster, he saw to it that the issue which had provoked the pre-emptive action stayed undistributed.[7]

To describe the rulers of the colony as a "family-company compact" was not hyperbole.[8] In addition to Douglas there was a council of three: the chief factor, the chief trader and the chief pensioner of the Hudson's Bay Company, all of whom met in secret. In the House of Assembly were to be found Douglas' son-in-law, the clerk of the company, three retired officers of the company and the agent of the Puget Sound Agricultural Company, which was a Hudson's Bay Company subsidiary. This close group of loyal colleagues, working together, constituted as watertight, secretive and authoritarian an administration as any opponent of representative government could wish for, and De Cosmos maintained an attack on Douglas and his government that was relentless and vivid. "It was," he wrote, "a wizened contrivance which kept its doors so closed to the refreshing popular breeze that it has become asthmatic."

As the editor of a thriving newspaper, De Cosmos could be expected to be in favour of freedom of the press. But it was not simply for personal gain that he advocated time and again this freedom. When he learned that it was being mooted in England that all restrictions of freedom of the press were to be removed, he immediately called for the same in the two colonies, at the same time noting that it was unlikely: "If these long obsolete gag-statutes of England, should be abolished, as by this time they probably have been, we wonder if His Excellency Gov. Douglas, by whose arbitrary edict they were revived and enforced in this country, will deem a special act of Parliament necessary to render them null in this colony."[9] The sarcasm was telling.

⚮

Before turning to the study of De Cosmos as a politician, it is important to remember that from the beginning of his time as editor, De Cosmos brought a clear-sightedness and vigour as well as his trenchant style to a range of social issues. A typical example is when the legislature, backed by Douglas, attempted to prevent the Jews from being naturalized. This rejection of the Jews was established in the Aliens Act of March 1859, which De Cosmos criticized strongly, saying that Douglas should "remember how unfortunate it is for this, a young Colony of England, destined to be the emporium of nations, to have the stain of religious bigotry and persecution fashioned on it."[10] The act was changed.

He also fought against attempts to create an established church in the colony. Having gleaned from the *Christian*

Guardian that Douglas was planning to put Crown lands at the disposal of the church whenever it was required, De Cosmos insisted that "voluntary aid is the source to which religion ought to look for support, and government assistance should be frowned down by everyone, who wishes the country to escape mixing religion with our politics."[11]

He was particularly opposed to the attempt by the state to force the Christian religion on the First Nations. "If the government intends to aid the Indians, let the aid be given without holding a blanket in one hand and the thirty-nine articles in the other. Let religion work its way among the Indians on the voluntary principle, as it does among us.... Let missionary enterprises have the sanction of the church and not the state."[12] Later governments might well have looked to De Cosmos for the position he took on the issue of First Nations and religion when they instituted residential schools through the churches, as the example of Father Brabant on Meares Island dramatically illustrates.[13]

 espo

A theatrical event of the kind De Cosmos revelled in, and which added to his notoriety among Victoria's establishment, came about through the involvement of another of the colourful characters who strode through the business and political life of Victoria in the 1860s. Alfred Penderell Waddington was a member of a wealthy English family who owned and managed cotton spinning mills on the River Avre, southwest of Paris. Before managing the mills, Waddington had studied commerce in France and had attended university in Germany.

As the phrase runs, he was a man of many parts. Approaching fifty, he was overcome with wanderlust and set off for the New World, stopping briefly in Brazil and then settling for a time in San Francisco where, with his managerial skills, he became the member of a wholesale grocery firm. In 1858, he was sent to open a branch in Victoria, arriving there in the same month as De Cosmos.

His commercial background, education, adventurousness and convivial habits, together with the fact that he was also a bachelor, a man reform-minded in his views and an outspoken critic of Governor Douglas, made him an acquaintance with whom De Cosmos could feel kinship and ease. Their common experience in the wholesale grocery business was a further bond. It was the nearest De Cosmos came to a sustained relationship.

In 1859, Waddington produced a work entitled *The Necessity for Reform* (the first published book in the colony), in which he called for less restrictive voting qualifications and a change in the composition of the island's Executive Council. When, at the age of sixty, Waddington offered himself as a reform candidate for the island assembly, he was duly returned and the friendship was further strengthened.

It was natural, therefore, that, in private sessions of gossip and tipple, Waddington should regale De Cosmos with the woeful tales of an elected representative. Whatever their inner drives, both men were serious in their concern for good government and, when sessions of the assembly had to be adjourned, as often happened because the number of representatives attending the Beacon Hill Park racetrack made a

Alfred P. Waddington, 1864. [BCPA A 01885]

quorum impossible, they were incensed. On one such occasion, Dr. Helmcken, as Speaker of the House, had refused to
adjourn the assembly to allow government estimates to be
debated in committee for fear that there would be no government majority in attendance. When Waddington gave De
Cosmos a full account of the event, the response was one of
De Cosmos' more graphic denunciations:

> So he, the Speaker, the son-in-law of the Governor, who
> boasted that he would bend the House to his policy, tries it
> by refusing to leave the chair...according to parliamentary
> usage, according to the dignity and decorum and order of the
> House. Such conduct shows what he is, what disgraceful

shifts dishonest policy entails, and how impossible it is for such as he and his kind to exert any moral influence in an intelligent country.[14]

This was too much for the Speaker and his cohorts, and the Sergeant-at-Arms was dispatched to bring De Cosmos to the bar of the House to explain himself and to apologize. Woodcock devotes an amusing paragraph to the picture of De Cosmos charging down Government Street, flailing his walking stick as he strode across James Bay Bridge to the legislature with the Sergeant panting doggedly behind him.[15]

At the bar he made a tepid expression of regret, moderating it still further with the typically risible claim that "no man in this colony has less vindictiveness than I have...." This was not enough for the affronted, and they demanded a full apology. He was not cowed. "I apologize for the publication of an article which I believed to be based on correct information." And, with that, he left the chamber, warning the government soon after this incident that, if there were any further attempts to gag a free press, he would express his views in a newspaper that would appear daily instead of three times a week. Not only did he carry out the threat but, by 1862, he had raised the circulation of the *British Colonist* from the initial two hundred to four thousand copies.

After little more than two years in the editor's chair, De Cosmos found it too constricting for the role he had assumed, and he made his long-intended move to the political stage, only to be frustrated, as he might have anticipated, by the personalities and strategies he had been attacking.

CHAPTER 7

Entering the
Political Arena

In a roughly furnished room, twenty feet long and twelve feet
wide, in a log building within the barricades of Fort Victoria,
seven men who comprised the first Legislative Assembly of
Vancouver Island held their opening session in August 1856.
That was the meeting at which Helmcken was chosen as
Speaker. Two years later the assembly moved to another
room in the fort where it continued to be one of the Speaker's
duties on cold days to light the fire in the room's dilapidated
wood stove. Helmcken recalled the events on one such occasion. It was a June morning in 1858 when, "...to my alarm, a
real, expectant audience appeared, i.e. a glossy stovepipe hat,
with a black-haired, dark-eyed, thin-visaged, spare and well-

clothed gentleman under it, who said in measured tones, 'If I were Mr. Speaker, I would soon have a decent place of meeting, and someone to light the fire.'"[1] This event is significant in that, occurring as it did barely a month after De Cosmos' abortive trip to the mainland and before he had started the *British Colonist*, it was the first outward sign that he had begun to take an interest in what was to become a total immersion in the island's political life. It was also an early sign that, whatever careers he eventually followed, courtesy and humility were not likely to be his hallmark.

CONFRONTING CLASS

In his years as a journalist, conflict between De Cosmos and the ruling clique in Victoria largely meant an exchange of insults and accusations, marinated in spicy badinage. The collective opinion expressed by the substantial and influential coterie of Anglo-colonial persuasion in Victoria was that De Cosmos was a semi-Yankee adventurer, a man of no breeding, a scurrilous scribe and rabble-rouser, an agitator. For his part, De Cosmos regarded purposeful agitation as his calling and showed himself as a foe of unearned privilege and of the "family-company compact" that, he asserted, presumed to rule the island. He met their pretensions with his own brand of disdain. They and those who aspired to be part of their circle were "our parvenu aristocracy," and most of them, he said, in what should be one of his more memorable phrases, "might take a mushroom for a coat of arms."

It was a theatre of taunts rather than threats. Once he announced his intention of becoming a player in the arena where

John S. Helmcken, c. 1895. [BCPA A-01349]

it really counted, the atmosphere changed. Political power on the island had been exercised by the representatives and off-shoots of a British upper class tradition who were not only convinced of their superior right and capacity to rule but also of their right to exercise the art of social and, if necessary, political exclusion. When De Cosmos threatened to invade their power structure, they became ruthless in their attempts to keep the upstart out.

As with all discussions of class there are complications. Any description of the class-conscious society of Victoria of the time has to take into account the fact that, by demographic necessity, if no other, mixed marriages were prevalent at every level of Victorian society, and quite markedly so among many of its leading citizens. A further complication, specific to Victoria, was that, at the top of the social pyramid, such as it was, stood a man who had considerable, even historic achievements to his credit, but who was not only the offspring of his father and a woman of mixed European and African ancestry but was himself the partner in a mixed marriage and therefore in no sense a member of the elite — in the starched meaning of that term.

By dint of steady application, Douglas had learned to prac-tise and display the effortless authority, the physical bearing and the forms of speech that the position was thought to re-quire, first as chief factor of the Hudson's Bay Company and then as governor. The cost of maintaining that kind of poise, however, was that he possessed a persona as inwardly con-strained in its way as was De Cosmos in his. Douglas had a reputation for disdainful behaviour to "inferiors" and a curtness of manner that made it difficult for him to generate ease and warmth among those close to him. "He was a very self-contained man, rarely giving his confidence to anyone, and to me scarcely ever,"[2] writes his own son-in-law in his *Reminiscences*. It is not difficult to see both De Cosmos and Douglas as each other's *bête noire* and mirror image.

The relationship between Douglas and De Cosmos took on a still more complex and fascinating aspect following an event that happened shortly after the date of the governor's official retirement. In October 1863, soon after the news reached Victoria that the Queen had granted Douglas a knighthood, and De Cosmos was already retired from the editorship of the *Colonist*, an editorial appeared to which it is worth paying close attention in an attempt to determine its full implication. It reads, in part, as follows:

> We have conceived it our duty upon some occasions to differ from the policy pursued by Mr. Douglas as governor of the colony, and we have from time to time had occasion as public journalists to oppose that policy — we trust however that such opposition has at no time been factious — personal to the Governor it has never been. If we have opposed the measures of government we have never in our criticisms of the public acts of the executive head of that government failed in our esteem for the sterling honesty of purpose which has guided those acts, nor the manly and noble qualities and virtues which adorn the man.... His services to his country as Governor of these colonies will not be forgotten for many years to come, and we believe that nothing will be remembered of his administration of the government that will tend to tarnish the name of Douglas.[3]

Governor James Douglas. [BCPA A-03909]

Amor De Cosmos, c. 1865. [BCPA C-09025]

It is not known who wrote that piece, and opinions differ, but in the sonority of the phrasing and the extravagant claim to being pure in purpose and restrained in rebuke, it is not difficult to discern the hand of the very recently retired editor. How to interpret it? An attempt to help history explain and excuse the ferocity of his attacks? Or did the occasion suddenly cause a surge of human warmth to penetrate his protective armour?

Another event occurring at the same time may have some bearing on the question. In September 1863, a petition was being circulated in Victoria, calling on the Imperial Government to retain Douglas in office. It was denounced in many quarters as an attempt by the Imperial Government to keep British Columbia under a permanent governorship and, in his last weeks in control of the *British Colonist*, De Cosmos had written an editorial in which he joined in the denunciation. Remarkably, he did so in terms that were statesmanlike in tone and content. In the next day's issue there appeared below the paper's main editorial a statement, signed simply "A." The first sentence was "*Now or never* is the time to discuss the subject of the union of the two colonies, and to act upon it with promptitude."[4]

Taken together these two incidents serve to show that De Cosmos was both tidying away his own long-running conflict with Douglas and asserting that the Douglas era was history, that a new one had begun. By then, after a long-drawn-out attempt, he had finally won a seat in the legislature, and his focus was now on ensuring that in this new regime he would possess that position of prominence and authority he had promised himself.

THE CANDIDATE

De Cosmos' entry into politics was by no means easy or assured. He first ran as a candidate for Victoria in the election
called in January 1860. As a close observer of the political
scene, De Cosmos had become well acquainted with its hazards. Nevertheless, his first major foray into actual political
combat turned out to be more demanding than he had anticipated. And it showed: "De Cosmos appeared on the stage...
performed all sorts of semi-theatrical attitudes... boasted of
travelling through California with a revolver in each boot or
something of the sort.... De Cosmos was drunk."[5] That is
how Helmcken remembered De Cosmos' first performance
as a political candidate. De Cosmos' paper put it differently.
"His voice," it reported, was "rendered feeble by ill-health."

Although drinking played an increasingly significant part
in De Cosmos' political career, there was little sign of it in the
earlier years. It did not feature among his Halifax activities
(his mentor, John Thompson, was a strong temperance advocate). On the wagon trail and in Salt Lake City, heavy indul-
gence would have been unwise and, in any case, the supply
was limited. In the mining districts of California, it could
have been a different story. Smith, however, was at the time
engaged in the absorbing business of becoming De Cosmos.
In formulating and acting upon the newly minted destiny he
was shaping for himself, he was creating more convincing
fantasies in his mind than ever a surfeit of hard liquor could
achieve.

In his early days in Victoria, before the strain of adapting to
the pressures of public life overtook him, he allegedly saw
some virtue in abstinence. In fact, De Cosmos, it has been

asserted, was an early supporter of the temperance movement but, if this was the case, his focus and that of his newspaper shifted toward more political interests and aspirations in the 1860s.[6]

He was defeated in his attempt to win a seat in January 1860, first at the general election and then at a by-election seven months later. Although Helmcken claimed that this was due to his drinking, and while drink may have played a role, it was not the major cause. The decisive reason for the first failure was the sleight of hand engineered by Douglas on the advice of his attorney general, George Hunter Cary, who happened to be standing against De Cosmos at the same election. Recently a sizable number of Afro-Americans had arrived in Victoria from California. Cary arranged for them to be treated as voting citizens. He reminded Douglas that, in March of 1857, in the notorious Dred Scott case, the United States Supreme Court, headed by Chief Justice Roger B. Taney, had decided by a vote of seven to two, that all Blacks — slaves as well as free — were not and could never become citizens of the United States.

A group within the Black community of San Francisco, anxious to escape this oppression in their daily lives, had formed a "Pioneer Committee" with plans to emigrate to wherever they would enjoy the benefits of a more open society. Mexico and Panama were considered, but at a community meeting they were addressed by Captain Jeremiah Nagle, the captain of a British ship, the *Commodore*. Nagle, allegedly at the request of Governor Douglas, presented a glowing account of the prospects they would enjoy on

Vancouver Island. A representative group of the community sailed to Victoria on the *Commodore* to study the social and economic scene and prospects. They returned to San Francisco with a positive report, and the first contingent was soon on its way.

They rapidly established themselves as businessmen and property owners, many of them entering the retail trade in Victoria and, as sign of their commitment, organized a volunteer rifle corps.[7] Cary had persuaded Douglas that, as the members of this Black community of Victoria were no longer (if they ever had been) American citizens, any Black man possessing the very loose property requirements should be encouraged to swear allegiance to the Queen and acquire the vote.

De Cosmos made no immediate protest, probably thinking that he might gain the Black vote himself. In the event, they expressed their gratitude by voting solidly for Cary and Selim Franklin, another company man, and De Cosmos was defeated. In March of the following year, it was found that this had been an illegal arrangement. Their citizenship rights were withdrawn and their names were removed from the voters list. As far as De Cosmos was concerned, however, the damage had been done and he deployed his customary anger against the Douglas-Cary subterfuge. His attitude to the action of the Black community was first to express himself in terms of tolerance and understanding, and then to let himself go with all the fury he could muster. In an editorial a few days after the election, he wrote:

The colored people who have...controlled the election are not the only parties to blame. Coming hither from a country where no rights are conceded to them, it is quite natural that they should eagerly accept every privilege offered them.[8]

De Cosmos asserted that while the Dred Scott case meant they were denied American citizenship, they were still foreigners. "Though disenfranchised, they are still Americans." A week later he made plain his real feelings — and his guile. A long letter appeared, written in an immediately recognizable style but under the pseudonym of "Shears":

> The truth is — and the sooner it is told the better — the colored people do not know what are their rights, and are not satisfied when they have them. They always want a little more liberty than white men, and if they can't get it they fancy themselves ill treated. . . . Acting upon the mistaken notion that freedom is without limits, they succeed in making themselves hated wherever they go. . . . Who, then, but themselves are to blame for the prejudices existing against them?[9]

This semi-anonymous communication allowed for a reply in which De Cosmos could not be directly attacked, but Mifflin Wistar Gibbs, the spokesman for the Afro-American community in Victoria, took the opportunity to counter with a strong but measured attack on the writer and his views. Gibbs was an impressive figure and was, as De Cosmos came to recognize, equally articulate and intelligent, successful in business and effective in civic affairs. Even though De Cosmos never withdrew his assertion, a degree of respect grew between them.

At the Yale Convention, which De Cosmos and allies convened to advance the cause of Confederation and responsible institutions, the Salt Spring Island's delegate was Mifflin Wistar Gibbs. Whether or not De Cosmos' antagonism had abated or been set aside, he was not about to spurn the involvement of "the coloured people."

In August of the same year De Cosmos made another attempt to win a seat, this time at a by-election in Esquimalt. The manipulation that ensured this second defeat was equally imaginative and equally devious. The government decided that an individual bearing a name registered in California was not eligible to stand in a Vancouver Island election unless he called himself "William Alexander Smith, known as Amor De Cosmos."

For once, and for the obvious reason that it would have been impolitic to protest at this critical point, De Cosmos accepted the stipulation and, in the event, was top of the poll by one vote. One man, however, named his choice simply as "De Cosmos." The sheriff immediately declared his vote void and, assuming a power he did not possess, duly cast a deciding vote for De Cosmos' opponent. Although that election was later declared illegal, the Hudson's Bay men in the assembly, wanting no part of this troublesome interloper in their midst, overruled this judgment and De Cosmos' opponent was still confirmed as the victor.

There was even more to this burlesque. The election had been conducted using an out-of-date voters list. The vote of the harbour master, for example, had been accepted even though his name did not appear on the current list. Then, in what seemed an act of sportsmanship, the winner resigned and stood again. To avert any possible danger, however, the earlier list was used once more, and De Cosmos' opponent was again returned. It was later discovered that, after all, he was not qualified to stand as a candidate. Later still, he was forced from office for embezzlement.

After both events, the De Cosmos capacity for bitterness and anger was unconfined. After the first election, he had railed against "the Yankee principle of ... ignorant foreigners in the hands of demagogues, casting illegal votes." After the second, he claimed to hear the people of Vancouver Island asking, "How long will such iniquitous proceedings go un-whipt of justice?" He had more success fighting for press freedom than he had in securing fair elections, at least at this point in his career.

ᴄᴢ

During this period, De Cosmos engaged in a number of bat-tles with the Douglas forces that won him a sizable following in the two colonies. The first was over the handling of Vic-toria as a free port. The colony was generally in favour of the proposal but there was much resentment when it was ushered in, not as a bill in the assembly, but as a proclamation from Governor Douglas himself. De Cosmos brought the full force of his sarcasm against such autocratic designs. "In the present day, when colonial self-government is so thoroughly established, that what formerly was done by proclamation is now done by legislation; we take it as no compliment, that this colony should be made an exception."[10] The free port issue was to return as a highly contentious topic.

Shortly after this, the mainland colony of British Columbia became incensed when Douglas imposed a £5 mule-load
tax. While the general population supported a small tax to
help build roads, the £5 tax seemed excessive. De Cosmos
declaimed that Douglas studied "the best mode to repel population."[11] In fact the Hudson's Bay Company had always
been more interested in preserving its fur-trade sources than
in bringing in immigrants. Interesting enough, De Cosmos,
through his editorials, raised such anger against the mule-
load tax in the two colonies that in the end Douglas retreated
and told his officials not to collect the tax.

This retreat certainly did not satisfy De Cosmos. He
claimed, "The imperious ruler of that misgoverned country
must feel lowered in his own estimation considerably, when
convinced that he dare not execute the mule ukase; but as a
statesman, how much lower does he stand when he resorts to
the unstatesmanlike shift of ordering the non-execution of
his edict. How much higher would he have stood had he ex-
hibited some degree of condescension, and publicly repealed
that which the united voice of the country has characterized
as infamous."[12]

Another of the issues which gained De Cosmos increasing
support amongst the colonists was his repeated attacks on the
government's handling of accounts. There had long been a
question of whether the Hudson's Bay Company owed money
to the colony or whether the colony owed it to the company.
Finally the assembly was able to gain enough support
amongst the reformers that a bill was passed to "consider all

accounts before approving the estimates." In the end, little came of this bill with the Attorney General Cary first stonewalling the bill and then resigning, so that the matter was left in limbo.

One of De Cosmos' great advantages in winning citizens to his reforming platform (in addition to his trenchant use of language) was his ability to see into local issues the larger constitutional principles. Thus, often what might have remained a merely local matter took on the hues of a much larger issue in De Cosmos' editorials. For example, in the fall of 1860 the council made it known that they intended to amend a liquor bill. De Cosmos saw immediately that this involved a surrender by the Lower House of their most important duty, the right to taxation.

De Cosmos pointed out that "Taxation without representation severed the old Colonies from the Mother Country. If attempted here...it may bring about such a combination as may rid the country of an irresponsible Council and an arbitrary Governor."[13] A long battle ensued between the council and the assembly, with neither side being able to bring about a conclusion, with the result that De Cosmos came to be seen in the eyes of many as a fighter for true, responsible government.

✐

The three years from 1860 to 1863 was an unacceptably long time in the political shadows for a man hurriedly seeking a real power base, but his stinging articles about the need for a change were clearly improving his political prospects. As a result of the increase in the size of its population, Victoria was assigned four seats prior to the general election of July 1863, and, at the count, a Douglas man polled the largest number of votes with De Cosmos in second place. He had finally secured a seat, having canvassed with a manifesto of no less than twenty-six points.

The increase in the number of eligible voters and an expanding audience before whom he could display his histrionic talent, all seemed to assure him of a permanent part on the political stage. The theatre would both dim and darken on him, however, before the end of the run.

It only took him three months in office to decide that he would give up the ownership of the *British Colonist* and devote himself full-time to the exercise of political power. It also provided him with one more opportunity for the histrionic gesture:

> So marked on some occasions has the support of the friends and patrons of the paper been, that it is with a pang of regret I now dissolve the connection and bid them farewell, in all probability never again to renew my connection with the public as the editor and proprietor of a newspaper....Nothing but delicate health, arising from over-application of the duties of a laborious profession, has induced me to retire.[14]

Opponents searched in vain for any sign of any diminution in his physical powers or in his zestful use of a telling phrase. It had been apparent, however, that the paper was in need of a new owner. David Higgins came to the rescue. Higgins had earlier accepted De Cosmos' invitation to join the staff of the

British Colonist but soon objected to some of the proprietor's editorial wiles and he resigned. Subsequently, as owner of the *Victoria Daily Chronicle*, he acquired the *British Colonist* and rebranded the two titles as the *Daily British Colonist*, a formidable organ of opinion, with De Cosmos as one of its principal targets.

The continuous presence of this influential adversary forced De Cosmos to create a new title of his own and, seven years after he had resigned from the *British Colonist*, he became the owner and, for a time, editor of the *Victoria Daily Standard*.

Having fully convinced himself that it was in the world of political influence and political action that his destiny lay, he immersed himself in it with such single-minded commitment and assurance that, within weeks of his election, he could be seen taking the role of chief critic of current policies and the leading proponent of radical change. His political career proceeded on its unpredictable way.

THE TASK OF BEING REASONABLE

The Initiative, Referendum and Recall are devices designed to anticipate, annul, modify or in some other way influence choices made through the normal electoral process. While they have a long history along the western seaboard region of North America, it was a long time before British Columbia officially aligned itself with that tradition.[15]

In its crudest form, however, the initiative existed in Victoria at a very early stage in its history. It took the form of proposals or policy changes demanded by public meetings.

Auditoriums were the venues of large gatherings, often eight hundred and a thousand strong, called into being, sometimes by a politically motivated faction, but often by a group within the general populace who were dissatisfied with the way those in authority were treating some matter of public concern. Confederation, a railway, a dry dock, the civil list, a governor's residence, all were found fit matters for public initiative. There was a hint of the *ad hoc* Athenian assembly about these gatherings, with the Victoria Theatre and the Philharmonic Hall as the *agora* of the period.

At one meeting, implacable political foes, accompanied by their supporters, would battle across the footlights. At another, they would be found standing, shoulder to unsteady shoulder, defending a legislative decision they had both agreed on, but one which had stirred the *vox populi* to expressions of anger.

While De Cosmos had been an editor and was now a professional politician, he also had, in effect, a third life, that of the public performer. It was a role in which he displayed his theatrical talents to the full. Often he was the instigator of the event and, at all such events, he invariably gave the principal, and always the longest speech. On these occasions we see him as he most wanted to be seen.

In 1864, the Imperial Government was planning to require the colony of Vancouver Island to finance itself by transferring to it the ownership of Crown lands. The *quid pro quo* was that the local government would pay the salaries of colonial officials, the so-called civil list. Included in the costs the local assembly would be required to meet was that of providing a residence for the newly arrived Governor Arthur Kennedy.

De Cosmos and Helmcken, normally on opposite sides of any argument, shared the view that this would place an unacceptable additional burden on local resources. To cloak any possible discourtesy to the new governor, they had agreed in the Legislative Assembly that, in lieu of providing new living quarters, a sum of two thousand pounds should be made available for a public celebration of his arrival in the colony.

In making this proposal, however, they had misjudged the public mood. A great many citizens of Victoria, including the mayor, regarded this as an insult to the new governor. They called De Cosmos and Helmcken to account for their action at a public meeting held in the Victoria Theatre. According to the *Daily Chronicle*, it was the largest meeting ever to be held in the city to that time.

Opening the meeting, the chairman stipulated that no speaker should have the floor for more than fifteen minutes, the length of time De Cosmos normally took to clear his throat, polish his weapons and set up his ducks. The mood of the meeting can be gauged by the reaction given to one of the first speakers who was so little to the liking of the audience that their hisses stifled him completely. His response was to stride silently up and down the stage until his fifteen minutes were up.

When De Cosmos rose to speak, the hissing was again so loud that, in the histrionic manner he had perfected, he shouted at the chairman, "Of course, if you wish me to be gagged, I've nothing to say." Frustrated a second time, he folded his arms and, as the report put it, "struck an attitude."

A voice from the gallery, well aware of his past occupation, shouted, "Take his picture!" Of course, he had a lot to say — much more than his fifteen minutes' worth — and, in spite of continuous interruption, he gave a lucid account of the implications of the Crown lands issue and his wish, by voting as he did, to protect the public from further burdensome taxation.

When Helmcken mounted the platform, the hissing was again so loud that he immediately left it, declaring that he would not say another word. Another word was soon forthcoming, however, and he spent it largely defending himself against the charge that by his vote he had shown himself to be a traitor.

The meeting was, of course, the best available entertainment in town that evening, enlivened still further when one member of the audience tumbled noisily down the stairs from the dress circle to the stalls, before limping and swaying to the platform to put his question. Nevertheless, the purpose of the meeting was never lost sight of. A resolution condemning the action of the legislature was passed ("with one man holding up his hand in the negative") and a committee of three was appointed to wait upon the governor and to report the outcome of the meeting.

For all the frustration and abuse the evening engendered, it had for De Cosmos the vital components: a burnishing of the self-image; an issue he could defend forthrightly and against the odds; a public platform for a theatrical performance that was spiced with a measure of painless martyrdom; a gracious acceptance of the people's will, and a denouement that justified his stance.

An ironic sequel to the meeting was that the government met the cost of a new residence, consoling itself with the thought that the money "would be spent on the mechanics of the city," only to find that His Excellency had used the funds to purchase the already existing Cary Castle as his official residence.

THE FILIBUSTER

As a journalist and a public speaker, De Cosmos was independent, dogmatic, histrionic and rash; as an elected man of the people, there had never been any likelihood that he would change. All of these attributes were in play in another and more famous event which highlighted a seemingly drab piece of legislation. It revealed two, at least, of his less appealing qualities — his lack of a sense of proportion and an imperious insistence that a battle once begun must end only in his victory. It was also one in which he exhausted himself and may have shortened the life of his collaborator and the principal performer, Leonard McClure, a fellow assemblyman and editor.[16]

Local inhabitants who had been obliged to sell their land because of unpaid taxes had been given a year to redeem it, if they were able to do so. The issue before the House in early 1866 was whether this should be extended for a further year. The argument was that, through the failure of the bureaucracy, the owners of the land did not receive all the necessary information concerning the redemption process. At each stage of the continuing debate, De Cosmos had opposed the action because, for one thing, he argued, it put in jeopardy the rights and security of those who had come forward to buy the lots.

It was alleged that, prominent among those whose rights and security were put in jeopardy in this way was one, Amor De Cosmos, and that this was what lay behind his theatrical act. It was an easy jibe for the cynic to make, but because of the secrecy he built around his private affairs and the deviousness of much of his public behaviour, it was one that was frequently attached to reports of his affairs in general. In fact, his name does not appear in the record as a buyer of the real estate in this case. It is just possible that there had been a third party acting on his behalf.

Be that as it may, his protest was overruled, the proposal was carried and the council began the necessary steps to prolong the redemption period. De Cosmos was not to be so easily defeated, however, and, master of procedure that he was, he again intervened when the bill came back to the assembly, objecting that the council was exceeding its rights in initiating what was in effect a money bill. In this way he managed to secure the defeat of the bill — by one vote.

The matter did not end there. The deciding vote, it was discovered, had been cast by a member who had been declared a bankrupt. His vote was thus declared invalid, and the original bill was reintroduced. It was now within a day of the date at which the twelve months' grace would run out, and the new law would come into effect. The bill had reached the third reading stage, in which the rules allowed no member to speak more than once.

At De Cosmos' instigation and with the help of long

Leonard McClure, c. 1865. [BCPA A-02282]

passages read aloud and made up of relevant and irrelevant allusions, reflections, reminiscences, and with a jug of egg-nog to hand, McClure spoke from two o'clock in the after-noon until six the next morning. Then, armed with the same basic life-saving equipment, De Cosmos took over and held the floor until one o'clock that afternoon. At that point, the opposition conceded defeat and the proposed new arrange-ment — and the speakers — collapsed.

A persisting myth has made De Cosmos the marathon speaker, but it is clear that he had placed the main burden of the stratagem on McClure's back and larynx. Ten years his junior, McClure was the kind of colleague who seemed to share sufficient of his own beliefs and attitudes for De Cosmos to find him a companionable agitator.

An opportunistic streak that ran through most of Mc-Clure's professional life made him a ready collaborator in a number of De Cosmos' more dramatic interventions. Brought up in the printing trade, he had worked in Australia before making his way to San Francisco and then up to Victoria (and, for a time, New Westminster). There he trod a tortuous and self-aggrandizing path, first in the proliferating newspaper world and then — to the horror of De Cosmos — in the annexationist movement. Later he moved back to San Francisco to both marry and die within six months at the age of thirty-two.

The extent to which the strain of the filibuster contributed to his early demise is, of course, unknown. It is not the best tonic for a weak heart. What can be said is that the overall performance was typical of the impetuous, ill-considered and histrionic behaviour to which De Cosmos was prone.

CHAPTER 8

The Great Campaigner:
Triumphs and Disappointments

The two important campaigns in which De Cosmos took a leading part and on which his fame largely rests are the drive to secure the union of the two colonies, Vancouver Island and British Columbia, and the crusade to take British Columbia into Confederation. By tracing the role he plays in each of them, we gain some additional insight into his mind and motives.

UNION

This was the first of the two causes in which De Cosmos truly believed. Even before he entered politics, he was presenting the case for union in beguiling prose:

The act of union would sink for ever out of sight the prospect of two or three petty colonies on this coast, each bowed down with the weight of Governmental machinery like striplings encased in giant's armor . . . each as estranged from each other almost as though the sovereignty of each other's territory was vested in different monarchs.[1]

And again:

We have no sympathy with the policy that would institute or perpetuate petty provinces, where the sharpened intellect of their inhabitants prey on each other; where the colonial mind, doomed by Imperial legislation to a subordinate position, is still further doomed to grapple with petty politics, shut up with a small population, and shut out by provincial boundaries from a field fitted for its expansion and elevation, leaving little or nothing in common except a common nationality. . . . We go with the spirit of our age. . . . It is not an age in which we should borrow our models from a past and almost worn-out Colonial policy.[2]

There are phrases here — "where the sharpened intellect of their inhabitants prey on each other" — which, together with the alliterative allusions, have the declamatory ring of a Shakespearean nobleman in one of the history plays. The outcome, too, took a Shakespearean turn. It was a union in which the power of the two players, imperial and colonial, was unequal and in which the more determined contestant achieved less than he had fought for.

De Cosmos had long been a campaigner for union and, in 1863, within months of taking his seat in the island assembly, he had introduced a resolution proposing the joining of the two colonies in a legislative union. Not wishing to oppose the resolution directly, Helmcken had countered by proposing a federal union, knowing that this would be unacceptable in London.

The matter was not pursued at this point but when the assembly returned to the topic, De Cosmos once again proposed a legislative union of the two territories. This time, however, he added that, if this proved unacceptable, he favoured federal union. While supporters and opponents might have been wondering whether he had been vacillating, changing his mind or accepting a reasonable compromise, the move he made three months later should have made them more uneasy.

At his instigation, the island assembly, in October 1864, passed an omnibus resolution in which it called for the immediate union of the colony with British Columbia "... under such constitution as Her Majesty's Government may be pleased to grant...." This was a carte blanche concession and a major miscalculation.

In an earlier legislative proposal for the governance of the union, De Cosmos had advocated a two-tier structure. There would be an executive council, to be composed of both appointed and elected members, which would be responsible to an elected legislative assembly. If the council ceased to have the majority support of the assembly, it would be obliged to resign. This was clearly a step closer to responsible government.

When Governor Kennedy was reluctantly forced to take

decisive action towards uniting the two colonies, the carte blanche concession made it easier for the governor to ignore any proposal leading to a responsible form of government of the kind De Cosmos was presenting. Kennedy recommended instead that the union should be governed by a single chamber in which two-thirds of its membership would be nominated by the Crown and the remainder elected. De Cosmos was furious, even though the proposal was in part an outcome of his own irresponsibly expressed readiness to accept whatever terms Her Majesty's Government proposed.

For De Cosmos and those who shared his position, responsible government could only mean a fully elected government. And it was being blocked. Yet when McClure attempted to forestall these developments by moving that the original carte blanche offer should be withdrawn, the McClure resolution passed with one negative vote — that of De Cosmos. He was standing by his central position, which was that union was so vital to the prosperity of Vancouver Island that it would be suicidal to say that they would accept union *only* if popular representation was included in the terms.

This sequence of subtle policy adjustments was a classic example of De Cosmos being shrewd in analysis, convoluted in argument, subject to ill-considered interventions and yet, on issues that truly concerned him, basically consistent. It could also be cited simply by his opponents as the performance of a man who was politically unpredictable.

When the provisions of the Imperial Act were finally made public, they were found to call for the disbandment of the representative structure in existence on Vancouver Island and its replacement in the new colony with an enlarged legislative body in which appointed officials were in the majority. This was decidedly not what De Cosmos had in mind, but as has been seen, it was in no small part as a result of his over-confident strategizing.

De Cosmos followed the same practice in relation to the other key issue in the union debate, that of Victoria as a free port. His pirouettes on this topic were, again, dazzling and, at the same time, explicable. He had always been a staunch supporter of free port status; it was one of the twenty-four items in his first election manifesto.

Later, he even said he would support New Westminster as the new capital of British Columbia on condition that Victoria remained a free port.[3] Yet in 1865, as the economy of Vancouver Island began to suffer a depression (as a result of the drying-up of the gold rush trade and with a growing rural population anxious to protect its agricultural industry), a free port policy now seemed to De Cosmos to have serious drawbacks. He also saw it as a major obstacle in his campaign for union.

For the commercial men of the city, however, the free port was a boon and, in their view, economic disaster would follow if it was abandoned. To bring the matter to a head, and with that combination of recklessness, arrogance and political *nous* that was now endemic in the man, De Cosmos and a fellow member of the island legislature resigned their seats.

With McClure as his running mate he then fought a by-election in which they presented the case for the union of

Vancouver Island with British Columbia at the cost, if necessary, of Victoria's free port status. Another example of that subtle hedging that was part of his political style was his assertion in the campaign that he would be in favour of retaining the free port status if union was impossible — but in fact union was what he was fighting for. The election campaign was rough, with charges and countercharges of voter bribery, but the poll showed De Cosmos in first and McClure in second place in the final count.

Soon, however, the victory was to lose some of its shine. By the terms of the Imperial Act, not only was Victoria's free port status annulled but New Westminster became the capital of the new province. Union had been achieved but not in the shape he and many other campaigners for the cause had hoped for. In 1866, when union was officially proclaimed, there was little joy in Victoria, and even less in the mood of the man who had played a leading role in bringing it about. His spirits were slightly soothed by his election to the first session of the new assembly, although the prospect of working to advance the cause of responsible government in an assembly dominated by appointees of the Crown did little to reignite his reforming zeal.

The first meeting of the Legislative Council of the united colonies of British Columbia was held on January 24, 1867, and, for the next fourteen months, the one issue that threaded its way through all the council's discussions was the location of the capital city. John Robson, one of the most influential newspapermen and politicians of these years, with whom De Cosmos had shared both the closest of working relationships and the most bitter of differences, was a very determined defender of New Westminster's right to continue to be the new province's capital.

De Cosmos' stance on the topic, as previously noted, was ambivalent and, in the critical nine-hour debate of April 2, 1868, when the site of the capital was successfully moved from New Westminster to Victoria, his contribution was not significant. It was Helmcken, who had been campaigning hard during the previous months, who presented the case for Victoria. As the reports show, De Cosmos played a subdued, if touchy, second fiddle.[4]

His general mood had been gradually lightening, however, as the prospect of a campaign to take the province into Confederation took shape and gathered momentum. Although he lost his council seat in December of that year, he had consolidated his position as one of the earliest and certainly one of the most consistent champions of the Confederation cause.

CONFEDERATION

There were always — and there remain   differing opinions on the importance of the part De Cosmos played in the story of British Columbia's entry into Confederation. It can be argued that active campaigners like David Higgins and John Robson deserve at least equal recognition, the more so as working with De Cosmos called for an added resolve. There were those like Governor Musgrave who asserted that De Cosmos was motivated by the hope of gaining influence and emolument, and that his actual influence was to be discounted. To this charge, the answer must be that, in his earliest

John Robson, 1859. [BCPA A-01717]

editorials and in his first political manifesto and long before the prospect of gain, he was arguing that being part of a coast-to-coast Canada was an absolute necessity, both in the West's economic interests and as a means of defending its British heritage from US annexation.

Another view of the value of his role was that the interventions of any British Columbia politician or editor had little effect on an imperial government that determined such issues on the basis of calculations more closely related to imperial policies than to the aspiration of a new — if enlarged — colony. Whatever the correct assessment, it is impossible to deny that, in the campaign itself, the ceaseless politicking and that combination of relentless persuasion and indelicate and dogmatic manoeuvring that were his trademark were critical in achieving a successful outcome, even if it was not exactly the one that he had hoped for.

In the later stages of the campaign he nearly fell into an old trap. Just as he had shaped that loosely worded proposal that an immediate union of the two colonies should be "under such constitution as Her Majesty's Government may be pleased to grant," so did he seem to make a similar concession by petitioning Governor Seymour to take British Columbia into Confederation "...by such steps without delay as may be deemed by him most advisable." De Cosmos protected himself on this occasion, however, by emphasizing before-hand that any proposals would be subject to further consideration.[5]

Delay was one of Governor Seymour's favourite ploys. At the time of the proclamation, on July 1, 1867, which brought into being the Dominion of Canada, he had not yet transmitted the Legislative Council's petition to London. In the meantime, a different kind of obstacle stood in the way of the West joining Confederation. Rupert's Land continued to be under the control of the Hudson's Bay Company, making it impossible for there to be uninterrupted governmental control of the Canadian land mass.

Frustrated by these delays, De Cosmos decided to take the

case for the inclusion of British Columbia to the opinion makers and power brokers of eastern Canada. August found him arguing the case before the well-attended Reform Convention in Toronto. In a typical aside, he did not fail to mention that he himself had battled for the cause "for nine long years, often standing almost alone, with few to sympathize." Back home, he and his supporters requested James Trimble, the mayor of Victoria, to call a public meeting at which, as the leading speaker, De Cosmos would propose a resolution calling for British Columbia to seek immediate admission to Confederation.

It was the government's inaction, he argued, which justified this extra-parliamentary approach. Whether it was the result of fatigue, a fit of depression or a heavy tipple, he made a very dull speech. Nevertheless, the device of the initiative had been brought into play, and the resolution was passed. In the name of the City Council of Victoria, the Dominion Government was called upon to take steps to bring the colony into Confederation, "by asking Her Majesty's Government to instruct Governor Seymour immediately."[6] No caveats.

The mental strain of keeping up appearances was beginning to tell on him as he grew older. His uncharacteristically poor speech was one sign. Another was a series of long letters to the press which he wrote in support of Confederation. They lacked any of his flinty sparkle. Even so, they were a considerable exercise in public adult education and were one more segment in an elaborate, jumbled but slowly shaping set piece which became the basis of the province's accession.[7]

Whatever his state of mind, his determination never fal-

Governor Seymour, 1864. [BCPA A-01752]

tered. He tried, unsuccessfully, to move in the legislature an address to the Queen requesting British Columbia's entry into Confederation in accordance with the requirements of the British North America Act. Two months later, he and others formed the Confederation League, with the aim of bringing about Confederation "as soon as possible, and to secure representative institutions for the colony, and thus get rid of the present one-man government, with its huge staff of overpaid and do-nothing officials."[8] In the summer, he toured the mainland, drumming up support for the cause. In September, at the league's convention in Yale, he was instrumental in composing a resolution calling for a Confederation that was wholly in the spirit of and largely in the form of the proposal that the public meeting had made earlier in the same year.

His was not the only cause demanding the public's attention. The anti-Confederation forces were being buoyed up by a growing annexationist sentiment. A rough campaign was inevitable in an election in which he was a candidate and that was held only two months after the Yale Convention. One of the more innocuous sounding but subtly malicious taunts of his opponents in that campaign was that he was a bachelor, a man who was unwilling to offer hostages to fortune in the shape of children.[9] If it seems an odd form of vilification, it does at least suggest that they knew of no other form of masculine behaviour with which to defame him.

Because the anti-Confederation forces were threatening his electoral chances, De Cosmos attempted to keep the issue out of his election campaign, arguing ingenuously that, as the government had not opened negotiations, it was not a current issue and, in one of his rasher statements, he stated that the cause of Confederation was "dead and buried." This was another example of De Cosmos at his most ill-considered and impetuous. He quickly backtracked, explaining that his real contention was that entry on equitable terms could come about only when the actual terms were known: only then could the people see that it was to their advantage. These looked like the manoeuvres of a man not at the top of his form, fearing defeat and ready to employ any ruse to avoid it. A fact that excused him to some extent was that, so long as Rupert's Land was not part of Canada, the quest for Confederation was indeed in limbo.

Whether or not the opposition would have been strong enough in itself to defeat him, it was not put to the test. Governor Seymour intervened with a well worn stratagem. He was persuaded by anti-Confederationist friends to alter, by proclamation, the franchise in the Victoria and Esquimalt districts. The old qualification that voters had to be British property-owning citizens was replaced with a franchise that was extended to all residents, with the exception of those belonging to any of the First Nations and the Chinese population.

Moreover, registration and oath-taking were dispensed with, and Americans, who had little interest in Confederation and a great deal in annexation, were included in the dispensation. De Cosmos' defeat was a foregone conclusion. It dispatched him into another gloomy mood, and he stayed sullenly out of the limelight until two developments opened up new possibilities: Governor Seymour died and Rupert's Land became part of Canada.

Seymour's successor, Anthony Musgrave, arrived with an obvious mandate to advance British Columbia's accession. In November, a vacancy occurred in a Victoria constituency that was predominantly agricultural in composition and where the electors were more in favour of Confederation than those in the commercial sectors of Victoria. When a by-election was announced, De Cosmos became the farmer's friend by adding to his Confederation credentials his assurance that, if he was elected, he would fight to continue the protection of their farm produce. With the ownership of the *Colonist* now in opposition hands, the campaign was more than usually unedifying and acrimonious. Though he was elected, a stronger opponent might well have defeated him.[10]

With his long commitment to the cause, it was expected that he would play a prominent role in the Confederation debates when the terms of entry were being discussed. It is generally agreed, however, that, apart from his strong insistence on the necessity of an entry that was based on firm financial conditions, he played a surprisingly muted part. He was in another of his depressed moods, and its cause was both apparent and complex.

Given the history of the issue, in which he and his fellow reformers had battled hard and long, it was bizarre that the motion for union with Canada should be introduced by the nominated members of a council who, all the while, had been determined opponents of Confederation. When they had received a firm assurance that it would not put their incomes and position in jeopardy, they not only supported the proposition but themselves composed the resolution that it should be implemented.

In 1869, of the twenty-three members of the legislature, only five supporters for Confederation could be mustered. In 1870, all but three supported it. Even in De Cosmos' book, this was an unseemly *volte-face*. What was even more galling was that, as a visible and convinced fighter for Confederation, he might reasonably have hoped for — and even let slip the wish for — some appropriate public recognition. It was widely rumoured that the lieutenant-governorship was the reward he had in mind. When he was also passed over in Musgrave's choice as one of the three delegates who would go to Ottawa to negotiate the final terms of Confederation, there was little left to relieve his depression.

In the end, the delegation came back with better terms than had been expected and, on the day of Confederation, he both spoke at the ceremony and wrote a long article on the achievement that was celebratory in tone. It concluded, however, with a revealing terseness:

A delegation consisting of Messrs. Trutch, Helmcken and Carrall visited Ottawa last summer, concluded negotiations, and the Council, during its last session, unanimously adopted the terms of Union; and today we have become Canadians.[11]

Part of his subdued reaction could be attributed to the fact that, in spite of his most determined efforts, the passing of the motion to seek official admittance to Canada included no assurance that, with its adherence, British Columbia would be any closer to acquiring a more democratic legislature. In fact, when Governor Musgrave had earlier opened a new session, the governor made it clear that, while he was taking the lead in securing what he regarded as favourable terms for British Columbia's entry into Confederation, he would be opposing any provision that advanced the cause of responsible government.

It was no surprise that De Cosmos took strong objection to the governor's speech. While he had been ready to accept union of the two colonies without responsible government, he warned that it would be dangerous to secure Confederation without it. Even with the twists and turns of his political thinking and strategy, this was the one issue on which De Cosmos decidedly did not change his mind but stayed sharply focused and insistent. As a fighter for responsible government he had no peer. He refuted the opposition's argument that, in a fledgling colony with financial problems and a fluid population, responsible government was impractical and perilous. He also resisted the much-touted claim that it was necessary to exercise a degree of autocratic control in order to ensure that the populace was not led, unaware, into the annexationist net.

His hostility to Musgrave had already been fuelled when the governor appointed two members of the elected Legislative Council to the Executive Council, one of them being Helmcken, and neither of them being De Cosmos. It only intensified when the delegation that was selected to go to Ottawa to negotiate admission to Confederation also excluded him but included Helmcken who was, at heart, an anti-Confederationist. De Cosmos' continued exclusion from positions of influence, for which he was well qualified, was a sign both of the antipathy he aroused within official and elitist circles and — not unrelated — his own anti-social manner in the company of his colleagues. "He never could be genial," said Helmcken.[12]

Nevertheless, his many disappointments never deflated him completely. In June 1870 he had become a newspaper proprietor and editor for a second time. His new paper, the *Victoria Daily Standard*, proclaimed that he would continue to be a supporter of Confederation if its terms were satisfactory to the people. The first issue appeared as "an organ and ally of progress and self-government," and included both a strong attack on Governor Musgrave and an assurance that it would see "that the rights of all as men and citizens are not violated with impunity." It was in this issue of the *Standard* that, in his grandiloquent style, he called for a federal union of Canada with England and a "Grand Confederacy of all English-speaking communities . . . so as to belt the globe and rule the world."

In a new strategy, he called for a coalescing of all shades of opinion, regardless of former positions, "to create a party possessing the capacity to give force, vigour, direction, weight and influence to a popular — a people's — government."[13] The appeal fell upon deaf ears, largely because few had any doubt as to the person he had in mind to head this grand coalition. The more important and less noticed part of the appeal was his observation that the ever-shifting alliances and loyalties that determined policy making in the province was deleterious to good government. The time had come, he was arguing, to give greater clarity to public policy by bringing into being more clearly defined political parties whose policy differences could be more sharply distinguished by the electorate. In this he was ahead of the thinking of both his colleagues and public opinion. The *Standard* editorials on responsible government were relentless. It was the kind of pressure he employed best and enjoyed most.

∽

The Confederation Debate was also the venue for what was virtually the concluding episode in the long-running, if intermittent, interest De Cosmos had shown in the future of Alaska. His early and inspired enthusiasm for the purchase of Alaska had waned with the lack of interest that the Imperial government had shown towards the proposal and his own preoccupation with the demanding campaigns for union and Confederation.

In 1867, when the United States bought Alaska from the Russians for $7,200,000, there was apprehension in British Columbia, Ottawa and London that American policy makers would turn their attention to the prospect of making the United States a contiguous whole again, a concern that strengthened the case for Confederation.

With federation assured, the issue moved into the realm of fantasy. In the Confederation Debate of 1870, De Cosmos proposed, with John Robson as his seconder, that Canada should buy Alaska from the United States. In what must have been an atmosphere of airy exuberance, Robson then moved, as an amendment, that Maine should be included in the proposed land purchase. The legislative council did not, of course, adopt the resolution and the subject ceased to have any meaningful significance for De Cosmos — or anyone else.[14]

A fact which adds considerable piquancy to the saga is that, according to the archives of the Hudson's Bay Company, the Russians once offered the sale of their American territories to the company, but, as the ownership of land was becoming less attractive to it, the offer was declined.[15]

DOUBLE DUTIES

The years from 1871 to 1874 put an immense strain on De Cosmos' powers of endurance, which were prodigious, and on his mental peace, which was fragile. In 1871 he was elected to both the new Legislative Assembly of British Columbia and the House of Commons, to which he was also re-elected in 1872 and 1874.[16] Although the shape of the union was not the one he had hoped for, his election to the new B.C. Assembly was the culmination of a long hard battle. It meant so much to him that, in thanking the electors, "tears...choked his utterance."[17]

He then hoped and expected to be invited to become premier of the newly constituted province. Joseph Trutch, the province's first lieutenant-governor, had other ideas. Trutch was a man of wealth, strong opinions and influence. He was a relative of the former governor, Anthony Musgrave, and had been a member of the three-man delegation to Ottawa to negotiate the terms of Confederation from which De Cosmos

Members of the first Parliament after Confederation, 1871. De Cosmos is seventh from right. [BCPA A-04737]

had been excluded. It was no part of his plan to make De Cosmos premier if he could avoid it. He appointed instead John Foster McCreight, a man Trutch knew he could control. Bitterly disappointed, De Cosmos took himself off to perform his duties in the House of Commons, which he was finding increasingly congenial. The old trouper had achieved fame and influence on the provincial scene and was ready now to perform on the national stage.

One of McCreight's weaknesses was an inability to hold together the alliances and interests that swirled around him and, in December 1872, he lost a vote of confidence in the assembly. It was now virtually impossible for Trutch to overlook De Cosmos. He was duly appointed premier and, for the next fifteen months, he continued his provincial career in tandem with his more recently acquired responsibilities as a national politician. He was drawing level in achievements with his hero, Joseph Howe. A federal cabinet post would make the comparison complete. That was not to be, although before the opening session of his British Columbia ministry was over, he found that there were matters requiring his attention in Ottawa.

His was not a memorable ministry in the history of British Columbia. Perhaps his most enduring achievement as premier was his request to the lieutenant-governor to leave the room before the beginning of a cabinet meeting. By this act, De Cosmos put into practice, for the first time in British Columbia, the British parliamentary principle of the separation of powers, by which the Crown plays no executive part in the process of government.

However significant or otherwise his premiership may have been, it acquired notoriety as a result of his attempt to promote the province's economic growth by requesting the governments in both Ottawa and London to agree to what he saw as a better way of expediting the construction of the Esquimalt dry dock than was possible under the Terms of Union. In London, he had a cool reception.

Whether as a result of advanced warning or after a first encounter, British cabinet ministers either avoided him or treated him curtly. The only exception was the First Lord of the Admiralty, whose officials gave him more of their time because of his interest in British dry docks. The result was the modest grant of £30,000, payable on the dock's completion. From Ottawa he returned with an undertaking on the part of the Dominion government to provide a federal grant of £50,000 and a loan of approximately one million dollars at five percent to be used for public works in general (both currencies being legal tender).

This was to replace the original terms by which Ottawa had guaranteed the interest on a sum "not exceeding 100,000 sterling" for ten years from the date of the dock's completion. Although the proposed new deal changed the original Terms of Union between the province and the Dominion, De Cosmos returned to Victoria with what he regarded as a good return on his negotiating skills. In a matter of weeks, his career as an elected provincial politician was over.

An account of the events in the early months of 1874 is invaluable as an insight into how De Cosmos acted when under strain, both politically and mentally. Soon after he had

John McCreight, first premier of B.C., 1894. [BCPA A-01449]

returned from his travels, a public meeting was held in the Philharmonic Hall on February 5, 1874. Its purpose was to allow him to explain the proposed new agreement, an object he barely managed to achieve against the steady uproar in which the meeting was conducted. As with many occasions of this kind in which De Cosmos was involved, it provided an opportunity both to open an issue to public scrutiny and to provide a lively evening's entertainment, largely at De Cosmos' expense. The point of the one was often submerged in the boisterousness of the other, much of the latter being a reaction to his own public behaviour.

The meeting opened at 7:30 in the evening with some eight hundred persons in attendance, and it closed at one o'clock in the morning with a hundred stalwarts still present. There are two accounts of the meeting, and it is difficult when comparing them to judge how strong the support was for De Cosmos and the new arrangements. One appeared in the *Victoria Daily Standard*, which was now his paper, and the other in the *Colonist*, which, under David Higgins, his former colleague and now implacable adversary, had become the organ of the opposition.

According to the *Standard*, "Hon. the Premier entered the spacious hall...and was received with loud cheers." His speech was interrupted by "three or four noisy individuals... who kept the meeting in perfect pandemonium," and "a kind voice" called out, "Sit down, De Cosmos; they are afraid to hear you." At the end of the meeting, the *Standard* reporter heard three cheers for De Cosmos, "most vigorously responded to," and, for Helmcken who had also spoken, three cheers "that were very feeble indeed."[18]

The *Colonist* reported that De Cosmos "made his appear-
ance greeted by cheers and hisses," the latter loud enough
for the chairman to announce that he would take the names
of those who hissed. In three long columns, the *Colonist* described a turbulent and antagonistic audience questioning
De Cosmos' arguments and mocking his haughty manner.
They shouted "Mormon Bill," "How are you, Villiam?" and
"Schmidt," and "White-washed Yankee," while deriding his
frequent resort to the liquid refreshment at his side.

His response was to call those intent on heckling him "the
vilest scum of the earth, dross, lowest types of humanity ... his
voice sounding more like the shriek of the maniac, the last cry
of a despairing soul about to be engulphed [sic] for ever."
Supporters of his steady opponent, Dr. Helmcken, managed
to put their man on the platform where, according to the *Colonist*, "he was cheered for five minutes." There were cheers
and a tiger for Helmcken and three groans for De Cosmos
"who again resorted to the tumbler."[19]

Two days later, while De Cosmos was engaged in the legislature, another meeting was held in the same hall. It was
called specifically to denounce the agreement. Emphasizing
the contrast with the earlier meeting, Higgins, one of the
organizers, declared it to be "the largest and most respectable
meeting ever to be held in the province." It formulated and
passed a resolution rejecting the agreement, adding that "it is
distinctly opposed to the Provincial Government interfering
in any manner with the Terms, or agreeing to any new Terms
offered by the Macdonald Government until the same shall
have been submitted to the people for adoption."[20] Apart
from the alleged threat to the democratic process, there was

also the fear, expressed by the business community, that changes in the terms might put in jeopardy the city's prospect of becoming the terminus of the transcontinental railway.

As the resolution was being carried, Higgins, who was present at the meeting, announced that, at that very moment, the legislature was in session, debating a resolution to accept the proposals De Cosmos had brought back with him from London and Ottawa. Higgins then moved that the meeting, headed by Dr. Helmcken, should proceed *en masse* to the legislature and present its resolution at the bar of the House, and *en masse* they went, "shouting and cheering while on the way."

A section of the crowd piled boisterously into the gallery causing a rattled De Cosmos to move, with characteristic impetuousness, that the galleries be cleared. At this point, "the most fearful storm of execration arose." The Speaker then left the chair and most of the members left the floor. Mr. Smithe, member for Cowichan, however, remained in the chamber and, according to the newspaper report, was apparently asked, in the middle of this melee, for his opinion on what the parliamentary authority, Erskine May, had to say on the situation. Mr. Smithe is said to have given it as his considered opinion that it was lawful for the people to present a petition at the bar of the House. At that, part of the crowd that had remained outside broke through a modest police cordon and occupied the assembly chamber.

Eventually word reached them that the Speaker would receive the petition at two o'clock the following day. With that, the crowd quit the legislature, formed a ragged procession and marched across the bridge to Government Street, chanting, "We'll hang De Cosmos on a sour apple tree."

The following day the drama continued. The resolution that had been approved in the Philharmonic Hall was presented as a petition to the assembly where it was put in the form of a motion and passed. In the course of this debate De Cosmos announced that he would be resigning from the office of premier and as a member of the Provincial Assembly. In 1872, the Dominion Parliament had passed the Dual Representation Act, which now made it illegal for an elected member to hold a seat concurrently in both a provincial legislature and the House of Commons.

While his action was, therefore, mandatory, the hostility towards him made this the inevitable moment for the announcement. An opportunity to camouflage the mixture of bitterness he felt was offered to him when a member suggested that he might change his mind. The reply was in character: "I never change my mind."

According to the *Colonist*, he felt so intimidated by the animosity both in and outside the chamber on the night of the "riot" that, given the lateness of the hour, "he declined to go home until a small *posse* of special constables were sworn in, and about daylight the 'genial and gifted' sought refuge at his residence."[21]

There is another way of looking at the events of that weekend. They could be seen less as an expression of provincial outrage at De Cosmos' plan to change a provision in the terms of Confederation and more as a carefully contrived strategy to destroy him politically once and for all. The elaborately planned and widely advertised meeting at which his action was condemned, and the subsequent surge to the legislative building, effectively to bring about his downfall, seems remarkably like a well-rehearsed, over-acted drama.

The Tuesday-morning leader in the *Daily Colonist* announced that "Saturday night witnessed a scene which few men in the course of a long lifetime are privileged to see — an oppressed and down-trodden people rising in their strength and wrath to tell their taskmasters that to remain longer submissive would be a crime!"[22] It matched the level of hyperbole Higgins himself reached when he declared at the meeting that "the conspirators were forging the fetters that were to bind us hand and foot."

It seemed to take a surreal turn when, within a matter of days, De Cosmos was re-elected to his seat in the House of Commons. In his campaign he had declared that he had no ambition to go to Ottawa again and that, were it not for the amount of abuse heaped upon him, and an opposition that was attempting "to drive him into retirement," he would not in all probability have been a candidate (or so his *Daily Standard* reported). But who believed the old tragedian? The note of pathos had a familiar ring to it. As a strategy for securing the sympathy vote, it could hardly have been bettered. The election was, however, a close-run thing. He won with a majority of four votes.

&

Yet another revealing aspect of these events as they relate to De Cosmos' manner and mind is the sequel which took place in the Speaker's room, where the beleaguered legislators had sought refuge. An enraged De Cosmos was declaring the action taken against his government to be a matter of high treason, to which T. B. Humphreys, a very articulate, if pompous, member of the assembly, replied, "Beware, Sir, that it be not you who is attained [sic] of high treason to the State." According to a participant in the argument, De Cosmos approached Humphreys and, assuming a tragic pose, threw back the lapel of his coat and, pointing to the spot where, as the eyewitness put it, "...in ordinary mortals, the heart is supposed to lie," exclaimed tearfully, "take my life," to which Humphreys replied, in terms of which few first ministers have been the recipient, "Take your life, Sir? You miserable caitiff, you are not clean enough for an honest man to spit on."[23]

But there was more to it than that. Humphreys, described by the historian Howay as "a ranting demagogue," had been one of De Cosmos' supporters in the long-running campaign for responsible government, but when De Cosmos became premier he had refused Humphreys a seat in his cabinet. It was a colourful illustration of the way alliances could form and shatter in the raw political environment in which De Cosmos lived, moved and had his being.

THE LAST LONG ACT

De Cosmos' years as an MP have not been of great interest to historians — and with good reason. The province was the theatre in which he had played his major roles. On the Ottawa stage he had only two parts of any significance. One was in the long-running drama based on the railway clauses in the terms of Confederation, the other an unsuccessful single scene based on Chinese immigration. While he had many other speaking parts, he was never a key performer.

He remained convinced, however, that it was in the larger sphere of federal politics that he would finally be able to exercise his talents to the full, and for eleven years (between 1871 and 1882) he took off for the nation's capital as often as possible, setting himself up in rooms in Russell House (eleven dollars a night and twenty cents for boot blacking) and planning his desultory campaigns.

With his background in provincial politics, a self-assured debating skill, a sartorial style appropriate to a performer in the Commons and with a less unusual name when set beside that of contemporaries like De Veber and De St. Georges, it might have been expected that a measure of fame and reward would come his way. It was not to be, and for a number of reasons. While many men have found that being dogmatic and egotistical is no impediment to a successful parliamentary career, De Cosmos' generally anti-social manner and his capacity for generating almost instant irritation meant that he was never an acceptable "House of Commons man." He aspired to a certain gravitas, but it was his own prefabricated brand and it was seen as such.

Moreover, his well-developed habit of dismissing opponents (and often allies) with measured disdain would be less tolerated in the setting of a Commons debate than it was in the give-and-take of the "Birdcages," as the legislature was called in Victoria. He put down one honourable member with

View of the "Birdcages," the old legislative buildings,
Victoria, B.C., c. 1866. [BCPA G-05987]

the admonition that "he was advocating that Punic faith that
carried one nationality down to eternal obloquy." Historically
telling but a less wilting riposte it would be hard to imagine.

Another reason for his disappointing performance was
that he had passed the peak of his powers. After the turmoil
and the humiliation he had endured in the provincial legislature at the tail-end of many rugged years of West Coast politicking, the fabric of the self-constructed image had begun
to shred and, in Ottawa, the unravelling continued. A Commons colleague described De Cosmos as being "in one of
those nervous conditions in which the House often found
him."[24]

From time to time he made astute and radical interventions, one of which has resonated down the decades. In 1875,

he expressed the belief that the public was in favour of the abolition, or at least the restructuring, of the Senate.[25] He also moved an address to the Queen, "praying" that, in future, governors general "should be selected from the public men of Canada."[26]

A subject of uncharacteristic concern was the reform of the divorce laws. Specifically, he sought the abolition of the practice of granting divorces by act of Parliament. He was persuaded to do this, he said, after observing scenes in the House of Commons where MPs were canvassed to vote for or against a divorce without knowing the circumstances. He argued that "relief in all matters matrimonial would be best secured by creating a court in each of the provinces with inclusive jurisdiction in matters matrimonial and with authority, in certain cases, to decree the dissolution of a marriage."[27] It stands out as one of his more warm-blooded initiatives. The issue fizzled out when it was ruled that this was a matter for provincial initiative on which Parliament had no power to act.

In a more spectacular gesture he sought leave, on April 8, 1879, to introduce a bill to provide for the peaceful separation of British Columbia from the Dominion. He asked for a seconder, knowing that he would not get one. He had proposed it, he said, to embarrass those members from other parts of the country who were continuously criticizing the province and treating it as an "incubus" and an "excrescence." The House was not amused. For all his attempted involvement in national affairs, he remained, in his manner outlook and interests, the provincial politician.

Admittedly, in the early year of the province's representation in the Commons, neither the atmosphere within the group of six who represented British Columbia nor their collective behaviour within the House was conducive to the effective performance of their role as members of a national institution. They were demanding, with unwise frequency and often at cross purposes, that the House of Commons pay more attention to the interests of their province, and the patience of central Canada was being tried by what, in a five-column spread, the *Ottawa Citizen* called "The British Columbia Embroglio."[28] Four years later, the Ottawa correspondent of the *London Advertiser* was still bemoaning "another large dose of British Columbia."[29] The persistence of the province's representatives had made them a collective bore.

A little coordination within the group would have helped their cause, but a parliamentary whip, had there been one, would have been powerless in the midst of the deep antagonisms and suspicions that beset them. Any overture aimed at concerted action was rejected for fear that one of the group, and most usually De Cosmos, was seeking to gain support for a move that would enhance his own position.

The animosity within the B.C. caucus was especially strong and long-lasting between De Cosmos and Edgar Dewdney. Their careers had overlapped in 1868 at a time when both were members of the British Columbia Legislative Council and where Dewdney was violently opposed to the principle of responsible government. It endured in another issue on which both held fierce and opposing views: the most desirable terminus for the proposed transcontinental railway. It was a difference which became even more bitter after Dewdney had joined De Cosmos in the Commons as MP for Yale in 1872.

Their differences, like those between De Cosmos and Douglas, were, *au fond*, more than political. A civil engineer by profession, Dewdney allegedly came from a wealthy background in Devonshire and arrived in Canada with impressive letters of introduction. He was, in the telling phrase, "well-connected," and, in Ottawa, soon became a close personal friend of Sir John A. Macdonald, who later set him on a career in Indian affairs, culminating in the position of Indian Commissioner and lieutenant-governor of the Northwest Territories.

In Ottawa, Dewdney appeared as a balanced, conservative insider who made De Cosmos seem a pugilistic, wavering outsider. And Dewdney readily played the part of exposer of his rival's iniquities. "There is not in this Dominion of Canada a man more double-dealing and deceitful," he declared, and added "I know him and have watched him — beware."[30]

Part of Dewdney's animosity was related to the Texada incident in which, it will be recalled, "in a manner prejudicial to the interests of the public," De Cosmos and others were accused of acquiring the rights to property on Texada Island, on which a large iron deposit had been found. The report of a Commission investigating the charge came out soon after Dewdney's election to the Commons.[31] He, and many others believed that its verdict, which exonerated De Cosmos and his colleagues, was a whitewash.[32]

In his more reflective moments, De Cosmos must have acknowledged that the virulence of Dewdney's comment was on a par with many he himself had made in the past by way of editorial comment. It was no help to De Cosmos' sanity in his later, disordered years to know that his arch foe was spending the remainder of his active years in the lieutenant-governor's residence in Victoria preparing to celebrate Her Majesty's Diamond Jubilee.

De Cosmos' much-asserted capacity for never changing his mind was seriously dented in an exchange with Dewdney in the course of one of those seemingly endless discussions on the transcontinental railway. Dewdney accused him of changing his opinion on the proposed Fraser River route. De Cosmos replied that Dewdney was referring to something he had said ten years ago, and he wanted to assure his honourable friend that the position he now occupied, compared with that of some years ago, proved that he was "a progressive and not a standstill politician." According to Hansard, De Cosmos added that he was prepared "to change his views every day of the year, provided he could make them better."[33] His critics were ready to say that he applied the same flexibility to his principles.

In July 1874, a rumour circulated in Ottawa that a fourteenth minister was to be appointed to the cabinet and that the Pacific province was to be represented. The press was numbed. The reaction of the *Citizen* ("We can hardly credit the report"[34]) reveals both the unpopularity the move would have faced in other parts of the Dominion, and the dark suspicion it aroused as to who it was that the rumour swirled

Edgar Dewdney, c. 1865. [BCPA A-04735]

around. In the event, the fears proved groundless. De Cosmos had always been a man around whom rumours of self-aggrandizement naturally gathered. They began as early as 1864 when it was bruited abroad that he had applied to the British government for the position of Colonial Secretary of Vancouver Island. When British Columbia became a province, the gossip was that he expected to be made its first lieutenant-governor. In Ottawa, the British Columbia caucus and others were convinced that he was working his way towards that cabinet post. With his capacity for self-deception and an inflated sense of his own importance, it is not impossible that he had himself set these hares running.

The subject to which De Cosmos paid the most continuous attention in his Ottawa years was that of the railway clauses in the Terms of Confederation, which were followed by the convoluted and often acrimonious renegotiations, in which the governments in London, Ottawa and Victoria were all heavily engaged.[35] In the Confederation debates, De Cosmos had played down the significance of the railway clauses, saying that the important thing was not to have a railway across the continent but to have railway communication in the interior of British Columbia.[36]

When he saw that the prospect of a transcontinental line had taken hold of the imagination of the populace of Victoria, however, he was prescient and artful enough to shift his position, and he engaged in his favourite ploy. A public meeting was called in Victoria at which he both supported the transcontinental project and proposed that a railway line should be built between Esquimalt and Nanaimo to become, in effect, its far western section. The Esquimalt-Nanaimo project became an obsession.

George A. Walkem, who had been attorney general in De Cosmos' administration and had followed him as the third premier of British Columbia, appointed De Cosmos as special agent in Ottawa to assist him in negotiations around railway matters. His manner and opinions, however, prevented him from playing a defining contribution. On one of his missions to London the British colonial secretary found him "a fearfully tedious man," and Walkem himself said of De Cosmos that he had "all the eccentricities of a comet without any of its brilliance."[37]

In spite of his denigration of De Cosmos' negotiating skills, Walkem, whose time as premier coincided with severe financial difficulties for the province, asked De Cosmos to approach the retired Governor Douglas for a loan. In what must have been a bizarre encounter, De Cosmos persuaded Douglas to lend the government thirty thousand dollars, with De Cosmos himself taking a two percent commission.[38]

Once, when the railway negotiations had reached yet another stalemate, De Cosmos announced in the House that, if there had been no action within three months, he would be "knocking on the door of 10, Downing Street," and, if no satisfaction was obtained there, he would "look to Washington." This was another of his flamboyant and counterproductive gestures. If, as some interpreted the announcement, it was meant as a threat to petition for British Columbia's annexation to the United States, it did not add to his or his province's reputation on Parliament Hill. When he realized that the proposal to build a line from Esquimalt to Nanaimo as part of the great national railway was in tatters, only to be replaced in time with a less prestigious light railway line, he and his constituents suffered the dismay that contributed to his defeat in the general election of 1882.

The other matter he brought to the floor of the House with more than his usual vehemence was that of the status of Chinese immigrants. His views on the subject were almost cer-

Cartoon with De Cosmos ejecting a Chinese man.
[*CANADIAN ILLUSTRATED NEWS*, 26 APRIL 1879]

tainly shared by a majority of his B.C. compatriots, but his expression of them in the context of a Commons debate appeared to many of his listeners to border on the paranoid. His diatribe against "the greatest pagans on earth," and his call for their exclusion from the country and, specifically, from employment on the construction of the transcontinental railway or as crew members in "any Canadian bottom," occupied ten pages of Hansard.[39]

He worried that, if immediate action was not taken, "mothers would yet hush their children with the wailing cry that the Chinese were coming." This was extravagant rhetoric, even for him, and another sad sign of his mental state. When he rose to deliver the speech, Sir John A. Macdonald and Leonard Tilley were seen to leave the chamber, returning only after he had sat down. Other members were observed sleeping in their places.[40] Whether it was a move to keep him within bounds or a recognition of his special interest, he was appointed Chairman of a Select Committee to which was referred "the question of Chinese emigration in British Columbia." His opinions shaped the committee's 1879 report. "Chinese immigration ought not to be encouraged," it said, and "Chinese labour ought not to be employed on Dominion public works."[41]

While the anti-Chinese sentiment existed almost everywhere at the time, the needs of the railroad prevailed and some fifteen thousand Chinese labourers were allowed into the province over the next four years to work on the railway project. The episode was full of such ironies. It was so well-known in Victoria that a large part of his income was derived from rent collected among the shanties of Chinatown that, at one election, his opponents called him the Mongolian Candidate. He was also party to the deal by which, on its entry to Confederation, British Columbia would receive both subsidy payments and parliamentary seats on the basis of population, the size of which had been highly inflated by counting Chinese residents as citizens. The final irony is that the end of his political career came with his defeat in the general election of 1892 at the hands of Noah Shakespeare of the Workingman's Protective Association, who was even more stridently racist than De Cosmos.

Another and perhaps more substantial reason for this final defeat was his prophetic view of Canada as a sovereign and independent state. Although he was born a British colonist, he did not wish to die, he said, "without all the rights, privileges and immunities of the citizen of a nation." This was too bold a concept for many of his constituents and too unwelcome a prospect for those Victorians for whom the British connection was sacrosanct. Together they brought about his defeat. What remained of the province's class structure was proving an enduring and unforgiving force.

In Victoria, stories of his state of mind had long made him a subject of rumour and speculation among friends and foes alike. After his retirement, his rapid mental decline was more than a rumour; it became publicly apparent. In his funereal garb and with a flailing cane, he could be seen walking the streets of the city, proclaiming his beliefs and denouncing his enemies. In the midst of this mental disarray, the failure of his last railway project continued to prey on his mind, and he was persuaded to offer himself once more as a candidate for election to the Dominion Parliament. He was in no fit mental state to pursue it, however, and he failed to receive the nomination.[42] His decline continued rapidly until it was necessary to appoint guardians to ensure his safety.

Behind his self-assurance, there had always been a need to know what others were saying about him. In his later years this took the form of a persecution mania. He suspected a conspiracy, directed not so much against his person as against his property. It is said he constructed barricades to defend his home, the last private place in which he could keep inviolate his long-maintained persona. If, as seems likely, his condition had been exacerbated by a major stroke or an accumulation of small heart attacks, the decline would have been relentless. He died on July 4, 1897.[43] The death certificate records the cause of death as cerebral hemorrhage.

Commemorative Sherritt
Mint coin of De Cosmos.

CHAPTER 9

A Summing Up

This narrative has been mainly concerned with describing how, in his years as an editor and a politician, De Cosmos made a major contribution to the creation of a strengthened British Columbia and a successful entrance into Confederation. It has documented both his achievements and the ways in which his political style affected the course and occasionally the outcome of a particular political objective. It has become only too apparent, however, that while he played a leading role in the critical political events of his day, and demonstrated a reforming zeal in matters of great social consequence, he failed to secure the degree of fame and respect he both deserved and expected from his fellow citizen.

Many explanations present themselves. One is that this was due to the machinations and influence of a power elite intent on demonstrating that he did not belong to what was seen as an established "British" genteel society. Another is that, in the public mind, De Cosmos appeared to be more of a maverick than a responsible legislator, and consequently not a man for whom they were inclined to feel respect. His many electoral victories seem to suggest otherwise, except, as has been seen, and with occasional exceptions, they clearly denoted approval for his stand on the issues at stake rather than on support for him as a person. Another is that his probity in business dealings was a frequent topic in the opposition press and, whatever the facts, they will have affected what large sections of the population thought of him.

The principal reason for the lack of appreciation and regard on the part of his contemporaries, however, is to be found in the man himself. An acknowledgement of the many negative aspects of his character and behaviour are essential for a fuller understanding, not only of his unpopularity but why he thought and acted as he did. That he was a difficult and complex character was the stuff of street and tavern talk, and there were many signs of it. One of the most apparent was his total absence from social life. He took neither pleasure nor participation in it and rebuffed any effort to draw him into it. The need to preserve his self-image did not allow him to lapse into informality.

As a consequence, there are few first-hand accounts of occasions in which the nature of his non-political life is revealed. One of the more extensive is that of Gilbert Malcolm Sproat.

Among other things, Sproat was a businessman, an Indian reserve commissioner and (in effect if not in title) British Columbia's first agent-general in London.[1] He spent time with De Cosmos both in Victoria and during his official visits to England. After their first meeting, Sproat remarked on the brusque manner of his new acquaintance, which he put down to "his secluded self-sufficing habit of life." He added that De Cosmos needed "a couple of bottles of Napoleonic Chambertin" in order to open up to the normal flow of conversation. He also observed that De Cosmos displayed a marked difficulty in establishing an equilibrium between his impulses and the control which they needed.

Sproat actually had considerable respect for De Cosmos, praising him particularly for the way he performed his professional duties, calling him "an unpretentious, most labouring, just and business-like official." Indeed, one characteristic that was apparent throughout his career was this capacity for application. He showed as much concern with the minutiae of government procedure as with a strategy for securing union. Other examples of this application abound. On the day he was calling for the committee on the terms of Confederation with Canada to be convened, he was also calling for the "Returns of the Road Tax in the various Road Districts." He was also asking the Colonial Secretary whether the Government intended to make provision for the payment of salaries of public school teachers. At the same time as all this was happening, he was also calling for papers and information on the appointment of two new members to the Executive Council.

His diligence was never questioned. His attendance record in the Vancouver Island legislature greatly exceeded that of any of his contemporaries. When he was speaking to prepared briefs the records show that he was invariably persistent, well-informed and conscientious. He despised and mocked inadequately presented arguments. One might conclude, in fact, that the workaholic aspect of his official labours strengthens the perception that he relied on work rather than on personal relationships to bolster his self-regard.

Observing the behaviour of De Cosmos in casual encounters, Sproat noted his habit of being haughty and unnecessarily rude on initial contact, but insisted that "there was no malice in his impoliteness." Sproat accompanied De Cosmos on an inspection of English and Scottish shipyards he was making in connection with the project of a dry dock on Vancouver Island. In the course of the visit, he noticed De Cosmos' frequent use of a brusque "interrogative habit" in conversation with strangers.

It was as if De Cosmos was intent on making his own self clearly apparent as the authority figure. This, together with what Sproat gently termed his "occasional irregularity of thought and aim," would not have endeared him to the British ministers from whom he was seeking funds. Sproat's shrewd conclusion was that "It seems that from an early date he had marked out for himself a policy and a career," which came into effect even in personal encounters. He also made a comment that should not be overlooked in any analysis of the character of De Cosmos. "Few ascribed to him humour."

Another although shorter account of De Cosmos in a

non-political encounter is to be found in an article by Beaumont Boggs, who became a successful businessman in Victoria and took an active part in its civic affairs.[2] Like De Cosmos, Boggs was a Nova Scotian. He arrived, a very young man, from Halifax with a letter of introduction from one of De Cosmos' relatives. Boggs found De Cosmos, at the age of sixty-one, "a very egotistical man," who had a habit of talking to him "in a very lofty or superior manner."

A colourful and revealing incident occurred at their first meeting, when De Cosmos told him that "the gateway to the Province was through the mines," adding that, "no man ever achieved success until he had been strapped" — presumably meaning short of money. At their next meeting, Boggs told De Cosmos that he had been mining in the Similkameen Valley of British Columbia and, as a consequence, had become "strapped." He turned to De Cosmos and confessed that his initiation into the ways of the West had therefore been accomplished.

De Cosmos' reply is an example of the bizarre turn a conversation with him might take. He seemed pleased, wrote Boggs, and "he assured me that I need never starve, as there were clams on the beaches, and if I could not cook them I could always find a Klootchman [a First Nations woman] who would do it for me."[3] This habit of an inconsequential response frequently appears in verbatim reports of proceedings in the assembly. It is an example of the "irregularity of thought and aim," to which Sproat referred.

What would almost certainly have contributed to the wariness with which the general populace regarded — or

approached — De Cosmos was his unbroken habit of wearing the same unchanging style of dress from his first meeting
with Helmcken in 1858 until the time of his retirement, and
later. In almost every photograph taken of him in Victoria
and New Westminster, he is wearing the same outfit: a glossy
stovepipe hat, white shirt with a high collar, worn beneath a
thick jet beard (which, it was rumoured, he dyed) with frock
coat, pants and leather boots, all in black. It was as though he
needed a disguise as well as a covering. Any visible hint of a
change in his manner, mood or intentions could be concealed
beneath the same gloomy carapace. With the addition of a
crook-necked walking stick designed less to aid his gait than
to enhance his authority, he gave the impression of a man of
power, to whom it would be wise to show deference. In fact,
the citizenry seemed to recognize that the air of "authority"
was more of a mask than a reality.

After he had become a frequent presence in the House of
Commons, the gallery correspondent of the *Ottawa Citizen*
commented on his unalterable commitment to the same at-
tire. He also observed that De Cosmos' accent "is not American, nor is it English. It is what I may call Canadian."

He was a lifelong bachelor, but this fact seems to have provoked little comment either in the writings of his time or in
subsequent biographical accounts, except for the casual assertion that he was too involved in his political life to consider
marriage. Moreover, one should point out that marriage at
this period in early British Columbia was by no means an
easy matter, as there were few available single women. In
addition, the makeup of the population was such that the

number of exclusively male households of various sizes and configurations, together with those of mixed-race relationships, outnumbered by a wide margin those formed by the marriage of a white man and a white woman.

In what has been described as a basically homosocial culture,[4] any man as taut in his human relationships as De Cosmos would be unlikely to find comfort in any of those more available forms of partnership. Celibacy and hotel living were frequently the most obvious and acceptable options. It is worth noting that, among the many disparaging and highly personal remarks made about him on his many public appearances, there is no record of any carrying a sexual innuendo, other than the false assertion that he had married a Mormon back in Salt Lake City.

Among the more widely noted of his activities were altercations with political opponents, which turned into fisticuffs with the likes of Roderick Finlayson, the Hudson's Bay Company factor, R. P. Rithet, a mayor of Victoria, and Robert Dunsmuir, the coal mining magnate. It was a propensity invariably invoked as proof that he was quarrelsome and quick to anger, both of which were true. The events certainly occurred, and it was clearly unbecoming behaviour from a leading public figure.

On the other hand, it could be argued that with a febrile undercurrent in the life of a raw and rapidly growing city, where street fights were endemic, where law and order was a fluid concept, and the prevailing mores were those of that homosocial culture, behaviour of this kind, reprehensible as it was, was not exceptional. Nevertheless, these street fights have become an over-repeated story in the lingering legends of De Cosmos' colourful life.[5]

The more serious aspect of these incidents is that the outbursts of anger and impulsiveness continued and became a warning of the more serious consequences to follow. They were also accompanied by the conviction that he was always in the right; "I am never wrong" and "I never change my mind" were two of his most revealing mantras (although, as we have seen, he did on occasion publicly defend his change of opinion).[6] The episodes did not improve his image in the minds of his fellow citizens, leading them to believe he must be hiding something. During the performance of a political skit at an entertainment in New Westminster where an actor appeared wearing a mask made up of two faces, the audience showed by their reaction that they knew immediately who was being mocked.[7]

Looking further into De Cosmos' personality and character, it is very apparent that he was not a man of few words, and the filibuster was not the only occasion at which he spoke at interminable length. David Higgins, writing in his later years, said that De Cosmos was "by no means an eloquent man,"[8] and the effect of his newspaper experience had been to make him more eloquent in his writing than on the public platform. He could occasionally take off on a flight of beguiling oratory but he could equally well be grounded in lifeless discourse. His opponents did not call him "the Great Bore" without cause. "The Great and Gifted" was a sobriquet De Cosmos' own paper bestowed on him, one which opponents in press and politics alike latched onto enthusiastically in the

The grave of Amor De Cosmos in Ross Bay Cemetery,
Victoria, B.C. [BCPA]

certain knowledge that everyone would know to whom it referred. Governor Douglas, commenting on one of De Cosmos' election rallies, said that "the poor fellow is said to be overwhelmed by the continued roasting he has had from the wits of Victoria."[9] De Cosmos was not the only politician of the day to be roasted, of course. Helmcken was also forced on occasion to step down from the hustings, but the way in which De Cosmos would strike his "attitude" in response made him even more a figure fit for satire.

Then there was, of course, his uninhibited fondness for the bottle. It stemmed from the discovery in middle life that it helped to reinforce the self-assurance and assertiveness that were essential if he were to maintain his pace and purpose. It not only aided him in difficult encounters but, for a man not given to geniality, it also floated him through the necessity for polite conversation as well as providing him with moments of sheer pleasure.

On the basis of the evidence of the way De Cosmos thought and acted in both his political and private life, what diagnosis would a professional analyst offer? While insisting that he had no wish "to trespass on the territory proper to the psychiatrist," Woodcock tentatively suggested in his biography that De Cosmos showed symptoms "observable in manic-depressive psychotics."[10]

A less psychoanalytic response might be to look at the young William Smith's change of name to Amor De Cosmos after he had left Nova Scotia and consider, for example, whether a phrase like "lover of the universe" did not eventually take more practical shape in seeking to empower people by fighting authoritarianism and urging the benefits of responsible government in the spirit of Joseph Howe.

The problem with this kind of approach is that while working tirelessly to demonstrate the virtues and necessity of responsible government, he showed little "love" for the individuals around him. He had difficulty consulting or working alongside the people he was trying to persuade of his vision, often straining his own talents and suffering periods of depression in the process.

A more fundamental fact is that he was basically a loner. We have seen that he was anti-social by nature, and there are many instances in his political career where he acted alone, showing little interest in alliances or coalitions. There was more condescension than empathy in his manner and outlook, and his loyalty was to issues rather than to people, even those directly affected.

It may be that a conclusive analysis can never be reached that will fully explain De Cosmos's enigmatic nature. It has to be recognized, however, that any catalogue of his problematic qualities, consequential as they are, lose much of their force when set beside his more significant record of clear-sighted purpose, relentless drive, and perseverance in the face of difficult social and personal challenges, and his lasting achievements.

NOTES

INTRODUCTION: THE QUEST (pp. 11–14)

1 J. S. Helmcken, *The Reminiscences of Doctor John Sebastian Helmcken*, edited by Dorothy Blakey Smith (Vancouver: University of British Columbia Press, 1975), 174.

2 George Woodcock, *Amor De Cosmos: Journalist and Reformer* (Toronto: Oxford University Press, 1975). It was George Woodcock's biography which first stirred my interest in De Cosmos, and I remain indebted to him.

3 Robert Kendrick, "Amor De Cosmos and Confederation," in George W. Shelton, *British Columbia and Confederation* (Victoria: Morriss Printing, 1967), 67.

CHAPTER 1: HALIFAX (pp. 15–24)

1 Noted in a statement by his brother, Charles McKeivers Smith, written many years later. See British Columbia Public Archives M/D35.

CHAPTER 2: WESTWARD (pp. 25–33)

1 McKeivers Smith, op. cit.

2 H. W. Brands, *The Age of Gold: The California Gold Rush and the North American Dream* (New York: Doubleday, 2002), 164.

3 For a short account of life in the city in this period, see Frank H. Head's article in the *Overland Monthly*, Volume 5, Issue 3, 270.

4 Peter E. Palmquist and Thomas R. Kailbourn, *Pioneer Photographers of the Far West: A Biographical Dictionary, 1840–1865* (Stanford, California: Stanford University Press, 2002).

5 McKeivers Smith, op. cit.

6 Among the writings about this trek, the following are particularly revealing: Herbert Eaton, *The Overland Trail to California in 1852* (New York: G. P. Putnam's Sons, 1974); and Alonzo Delano, *Life on the Plains and Among the Diggings* (Nebraska: Nabu Press, 2010).

7 Quoted in Reuben Cole Shaw, *Across the Plains in Forty-Nine* (Chicago: Lakeside Press, 1948), 65.

8 McKeivers Smith, op. cit.

CHAPTER 3: THE TRANSFORMATION (pp. 35–43)

1 Delano, 238.

2 Stewart Edward White, *The Forty-Niners: A Chronicle of the California Trail and El Dorado* (Yale University Press: New Haven, 1918), Chapter 5.

3 In one of their more exuberant exchanges Douglas called De Cosmos a "white-washed Yankee," on the grounds that he must have become an American to be able to secure a name change in an American legislature. On the face of it Douglas had a point, except that Sacramento's official records contain no evidence of a De Cosmos being involved in any citizenship procedure. His response was that it "was a malignant, envious, black-hearted lie." Joseph Howe would have been proud of him.

CHAPTER 4: THE TRANSITION (pp. 45–51)

1 See Susan Shaw, *Overexposure: Health Hazards in Photography* (Carmel, California: Friends of Photography, 1983).

2 The *Masonic Bulletin*, Volume 9, Number 8, April 1946, refers to this membership and his "demittal" and to a later, related event in Victoria.

3 Text entries in the property tax records of Oroville are to be seen in the archives of the Butte County Historical Society.

4 See McKeivers Smith's obituary notice in the *Colonist*, 11 November 1911.

5 McKeivers Smith, op. cit.

CHAPTER 5: VICTORIA (pp. 53–59)

1 "Amor De Cosmos: A Political Sketch" in the *Daily Colonist*, 15 November 1908.

2 House of Commons Debates, 1872, column 82.

3 A communication from De Cosmos to the secretary of the Victoria Lodge, January 21, 1872, Add Mss2, Volumes 164 File 1, BCPA.

CHAPTER 6: THE NEWSPAPERMAN (pp. 61–72)

1 For a detailed account of the early newspapers in Victoria, see an article by Hugh Doherty, based on a research paper written in the University of Victoria's Graduate Department in 1971. Available online.

2 *British Colonist*, 11 December 1858. Available online.

3 Helmcken, *Reminiscences*, 174.

4 Daryl Ashby, *John Muir: West Coast Pioneer* (Vancouver: Ronsdale Press, 2005), 160–170.

5 Margaret Ross, *Amor DeCosmos, A British Columbia Reformer*, MA History thesis (UBC, 1931), p. 20.

6 *British Colonist*, 1 July 1859.

7 The undistributed newspaper issue can, however, be found online.

THE DE COSMOS ENIGMA

8 Adele Perry used the pungent phrase, "a tightly woven fur trade cabal" in her book *On the Edge of Empire: Gender, Race and the Making of British Columbia* (Toronto: University of Toronto Press, 2001).

9 *British Colonist*, 7 May 1859.

10 *British Colonist*, 20 May 1859.

11 *British Colonist*, 22 June 1859.

12 *British Colonist*, 14 September 1860.

13 Jim McDowell, *Father August Brabant: Saviour or Scourge?* (Vancouver: Ronsdale Press, 2012), 341–361.

14 Quoted in Doherty, 6.

15 Woodcock, 60.

CHAPTER 7: ENTERING THE POLITICAL ARENA (pp. 73–97)

1 Helmcken, *Reminiscences*, 339.

2 Ibid. A different side to Douglas and his wife are shown in Eunice M. L. Harrision's account of her life as a young girl visiting the Douglas home. See Eunice M. L. Harrison, *The Judge's Wife: Memoirs of a British Columbia Pioneer* (Vancouver: Ronsdale Press, 2002), 27–29.

3 *British Colonist*, October 1863.

4 *British Colonist*, 16–17 September 1863.

5 Helmcken, *Reminiscences*, 178.

6 Arthur Tuttle Allen, *Forty Years Journey: The Temperance Movement in B.C. 1858–1900* (Victoria: privately published, 1981).

7 See Crawford Killan, *Go Do Some Great Thing: The Black Pioneers of British Columbia* (Vancouver: Douglas & McIntyre, 1978), 65–67.

8 *British Colonist*, 12 January 1860.

9 *British Colonist*, 18 January 1860.

10 *British Colonist*, 7 February 1860.

11 *British Colonist*, 9 February 1860.

12 *British Colonist*, 3 April 1860.

13 *British Colonist*, 24 October 1860.

14 *British Colonist*, 6 October 1863.

15 See "Recall and Initiative Act." Available online.

16 *Colonist*, 24–25 April 1866.

CHAPTER 8: THE GREAT CAMPAIGNER: (pp. 99–140)

1 *British Colonist*, 18 December 1861.

2 *British Colonist*, 13 August 1862.

3 Admitted by De Cosmos during the capital city debate of 2 April 1868. See the *British Columbian*, 5 April 1868.

4 See the above issue of the *British Columbian* and the *British Colonist* of the same date for a full report of that debate.

5 *Daily Colonist*, 25 March 1867.

6 *Daily Colonist*, 31 January 1868.

7 *Daily Colonist*, 3, 8–10 February 1868.

8 See Max Fawcett, "The Neglected Legacy of Amor De Cosmos" (Hazlitt). Online at www.penguinrandomhouse.ca/hazlitt (accessed 18 February 2015).

9 *Daily Colonist*, 4 November 1868.

10 For a detailed account of this election, see Margaret Ross, 124–125.

11 *Victoria Daily Standard*, 20 July 1870.

12 Helmcken, *Reminiscences*, 235.

13 *Victoria Daily Standard*, 20 June 1870.

14 British Columbia Legislative Council, *Debate on the Subject of Confederation with Canada*, March 1870, 145.

15 HBC Archives, Winnipeg, A/175/83, A/10/53/303, F/29/2/225/241.

16 For details of the elections, see F. W. Howay, *British Columbia from the Earliest Times to the Present*, Vol. 2 (S. J. Clarke Publishing: Vancouver, 1914), 333–335.

17 For an account of this event, see Woodcock, 136.

18 *Victoria Daily Standard*, 7 February 1874.

19 *Daily Colonist*, 7 February 1874.

20 *Daily Colonist*, 8 February 1874.

21 *Daily Colonist*, 10 February 1874

22 Ibid.

23 Ibid.

24 Quoted in Brian Titley, *The Frontier World of Edgar Dewdney* (Vancouver: UBC Press, 1999), 36.

25 House of Commons Debates, 1 March 1875.

26 House of Commons Debates, 8 March 1875.

27 House of Commons Debates, 22 March 1876.

28 *Ottawa Citizen*, 13 February 1874.

29 *London Advertiser*, 22 February 1878.

30 *Daily Colonist*, 20 February 1874.

31 Howay, 336–337 .

32 Woodcock, 150–153.

33 House of Commons Debates, 16 April 1879, 1259.

34 *Ottawa Citizen*, 6 July 1874.

35 For a detailed account of these negotiations see Margaret Ormsby, *British Columbia: A History* (Toronto: Macmillan of Canada, 1971), Chapter 9. One of the lesser known publications chronicling this saga is a carefully compiled document published, as the front page proudly points out, by Amor De Cosmos. It is little more than a bowdlerized version of Hansard, and whether it was an exercise in self-advertisement or a message for posterity, it was barely noticed. BCPA NW971B D296c.2.

36 *British Colonist*, 19 March, 1870.

37 Ormsby, 263.

38 See Walter Sage, *Sir James Douglas and British Columbia* (Toronto: University of Toronto Press, 1930) and John Adams, *Old Square Toes and His Lady* (Victoria: Horsdal & Schubert, 2001), 201. Both have a reference to this incident.

39 House of Commons Debate, 16 April 1879.

40 *London Advertiser*, 17 April 1879.

41 *Journals of the House of Commons*, 1879, Volume xiii, App 4.

42 *Daily Colonist*, 6 July 1897.

43 Whatever may have been the state of his relationship with the rest of the family before leaving Halifax, the attachment was never severed. It is likely that he made visits home during his Victoria and Ottawa years; the first child of his youngest sister was christened William Amor Simson, and, as we have seen, the relationship with his brother Charles was enduring, if erratic. And three nieces were present at the restoration and rededication of his grave in Victoria's Ross Bay Cemetery in 1948.

CHAPTER 9: A SUMMING UP (pp. 141–151)

1 Gilbert Malcolm Sproat, "Amor De Cosmos: A Singular Figure in B.C. Politics" in the *Victoria Daily Times*, 10 January 1900.

2 Beaumont Boggs, "What I Remember of Amor De Cosmos" in *British Columbia Historical Association, Fourth Report and Proceedings, 1929*, 54.

3 op. cit. 55.

4 *On the Edge of Empire*, 10 and *passim*.

5 See Harry Gregson, *A History of Victoria* (Victoria: Victoria Observer Publishing, 1970), 67. For the details of such an encounter, see Woodcock, 164.

6 House of Commons Debates, 16 April 1879, 1259.

7 Helmcken, *Reminiscences*, 236.

8 "Amor De Cosmos: A Political Sketch" in the *Daily Colonist*, 15 November 1908.

9 Sage, 343.

10 Woodcock, 74fn.

SELECT BIBLIOGRAPHY

Adams, John. *Old Square Toes and His Lady*. Victoria: Horsdal & Schubert, 2001.

Allen, Arthur Tuttle. *Forty Years Journey: The Temperance Movement in B.C. 1858 1900*. Victoria: privately published, 1981.

"Amor De Cosmos: A Political Sketch." *Daily Colonist*, November 1908.

Ashby, Daryl. *John Muir: West Coast Pioneer*. Vancouver: Ronsdale Press, 2005.

Boggs, Beaumont. "What I Remember of Amor De Cosmos," *British Columbia Historical Association, Fourth Report and Proceedings*, 1929.

Brands, H. W. *The Age of Gold: The California Gold Rush and the North American Dream*. New York: Doubleday, 2002.

Delano, Alonzo. *Life on the Plains and among the Diggings*. Nebraska: Nabu Press, 2010.

Doherty, Hugh. "The First Newspapers on Canada's West Coast." Online at www.web.uvic.ca (accessed January 2015).

Eaton, Herbert. *The Overland Trail to California in 1852*. New York: Putnams and Sons, 1974.

Fawcett, Max. "The Neglected Legacy of Amor De Cosmos." Online at www.penguinrandomhouse.ca/hazlitt (accessed 18 February 2015).

Gosnell, R. E. *British Columbia: Sixty Years of Progress*. Vancouver: British Columbia Historical Association, 1913.

Gregson, Harry. *A History of Victoria*. Victoria: Victoria Observer Publishing, 1970.

Harrison, Eunice M. L. *The Judge's Wife: Memoirs of a British Columbia Pioneer*. Edited by Ronald B. Hatch. Vancouver: Ronsdale Press, 2002.

Head, Frank H. "Salt Lake City." *Overland Monthly*, September 1870.

Helmcken, J. S. *The Reminiscences of Doctor John Sebastian Helmcken*. Edited by Dorothy Blakey Smith. Vancouver: UBC Press, 1975.

Howay, F. W. *British Columbia from the Earliest Times to the Present*, 2 vols. Vancouver: S. J. Clarke Publishing, 1914.

Kendrick, Robert. "Amor De Cosmos and Confederation," in George W. Shelton, *British Columbia and Confederation*. Victoria: Morriss Printing, 1967.

Killan, Crawford. *Go Do Some Great Thing: The Black Pioneers of British Columbia*. Vancouver: Douglas & McIntyre, 1978.

McDowell, Jim. *Father August Brabant: Saviour or Scourge?* Vancouver: Ronsdale Press, 2012.

Ormsby, Margaret. *British Columbia: A History*. Toronto: Macmillan of Canada, 1971.

Palmquist, Peter E. and Thomas R. Kailbourn. *Pioneer Photographers of the Far West: A Biographical Dictionary, 1840–1865*. Stanford, California: Stanford U. Press, 2002.

Perry, Adele. *On the Edge of Empire: Gender, Race and the Making of British Columbia*. Toronto: University of Toronto Press, 2001.

"Recall and Initiative Act." Online at www.bclaws.ca (accessed January 2015).

Ross, Margaret. *Amor DeCosmos, A British Columbia Reformer.* MA History thesis, UBC, 1931.

Sage, Walter. *Sir James Douglas and British Columbia.* Toronto: University of Toronto Press, 1930.

Shaw, Reuben Cole. *Across the Plains in Forty-Nine.* Chicago: Lakeside Press, 1948.

Shaw, Susan. *Overexposure: Health Hazards in Photography.* Carmel, California: Friends of Photography, 1983.

Smith, Charles McKeivers. "A Brother's Recollection." BCPA M/D35.

Sproat, Gilbert Malcolm. "Amor De Cosmos: A Singular Figure in B.C. Politics," in *Victoria Daily Times,* 10 January 1900.

Titley, Brian. *The Frontier World of Edgar Dewdney.* Vancouver: UBC Press, 1999.

White, Stewart Edward. *The Forty-Niners: A Chronicle of the California Trail and El Dorado.* New Haven: Yale University Press, 1918.

Wild, Roland. *Amor De Cosmos.* Toronto: Ryerson Press, 1958.

Wilson, Keith. *Amor De Cosmos.* Winnipeg: University of Manitoba Press, 1985.

Woodcock, George. *Amor De Cosmos: Journalist and Reformer.* Toronto: Oxford U. Press, 1975.

PERIODICALS & NEWSPAPERS

British Colonist
British Columbian
Daily Colonist
Journals of the House of Commons
London Advertiser
Masonic Bulletin
Ottawa Citizen
Victoria Daily Colonist
Victoria Daily Standard

ABOUT THE AUTHOR

Gordon Hawkins was born in London, England, in 1921. He has degrees from the London School of Economics and the University of Toronto. Following service in naval intelligence in World War Two, he held appointment with the Canadian Institute for Adult Education and was presenter of the CBC's TV and radio discussion program, *Citizen's Forum*. This was followed with executive positions in the Canadian Institute on Public Affairs and the Canadian Institute of International Affairs. After a return to university life, he moved to the United Nations in New York to become the Director of Training in the United Nations Institute for Training and Research. For his part in Commonwealth affairs, he was made a Member of the Royal Victorian Order (MVO) in a New Year's Honours list. His keen interest in the history of British Columbia, and of Victoria in particular, began late in life but has continued into his nineties. Gordon lives in Victoria, British Columbia.

INDEX

Citations of photographs are in bold.

Alaska, 12, 116–17
Aliens Act, 68
Anglo-American, 62
annexation with U.S., 12, 97,
   106, 110–11, 114, 136

Barnston, George, 65
"Birdcages," 128, **129**
"Blacks" (African-Americans),
   82–84
Boggs, Beaumont, 145
Brabant, August, 69
Britannia (ship), 48
British North America Act, 110
Brother Jonathan (ship), 49
Burnaby, Robert, 58

Carrall, Robert W., 113
Cary Castle, 94
Cary, George H., 82–83, 88
Cary, Lucius B. (Viscount
   Falkland), 18, 19, **20**
Commodore (ship), 82–83
Comox, 56
Confederation, 11, 12, 85, 91,
   99, 105–17, **118**, 125, 128,
   135, 139, 141, 143
Confederation League, 110
*Courier de la Nouvelle
   Calédonie*, 62

Dalhousie Debating Society, 16,
   18, 37, 40

De Cosmos, Amor
  arrival in B.C., 51–54
  bachelorhood, 13, 70, 110,
    146–47
  background, 15–18
  business ventures, 46–49, 53,
    56–58, 62–63, 90
  death, 11, 58, 140, **149**
  health, 33, 37–38, 47, 81,
    138–40, 150
  journey to California, 25–26,
    27, 28–33
  leaves Halifax, 19–20, 22–26
  name change, 13–14, 35–38,
    39, 40
  newspapers:
    British Colonist, 58, 62–65,
      66, 67, 72, 74, 77, 80, 89,
      90, 112, 122–23, 125–26
    Victoria Daily Standard, 51,
      90, 115–16, 122, 126
  perspectives on:
    Alaska, 12, 116
    Confederation, 11–12, 91
    divorce laws, 12, 130
    First Nations, 69
    responsible government, 12,
      18–19
    Senate abolition, 12, 130
    taxation, 87–88, 93
    transcontinental railway, 12,
      124, 128, 131–33, 135–39
    union of B.C. and Vancouver
      Island, 11, 80, 99–100
  photography, 17–18, 22–23,
    31, 33, 46–49, 51
  reaction to criticism, 92
  relationships with:
    Douglas, James, 64, 77,
      136
    Helmcken, John, 11, 92
    Higgins, David, 55, 122
    Howe, Joseph, 18
    Smith, Charles McKeivers,
      48, 51, 159n43
    Sproat, Glibert M., 142–43
    Thompson, John, 17
    Waddington, Alfred, 69–70
  social life, 13, 115, 142–43
Dewdney, Edgar, 131–33, **134**
Douglas, James, 53, 63–65,
  67–70, 76–77, **78**, 80, 82–83,
  86–87, 132, 136, 149, 154n3
  (chap. 3), 156n2
Dred Scott case, 82–84
Dry Diggin, 23
Dry Docks, 91, 120, 144
Dual Representation Act, 125
Dunsmuir, Robert, 147

El Dorado, 14, 36, 38
Esquimalt, 85, 111, 135
E&N Railway, 135–36

Falkland, Viscount. *See* Cary,
  Lucius B.
"family-company-compact,"
  67, 74

Index

Finlayson, Roderick, 147

First Nations, 56, 69, 111, 132, 143, 145

Franklin, Selim, 83

Fraser Canyon Gold Rush, 49, 53

Freemasons, 49, 58–59

Gibbs, Mifflin W., 84–85

Halifax, N.S.,13–20, 22–25, 29, 46–48, 54–55, 81, 145

Hall, Gavin D., 38

Hangtown. *See* Placerville

Helmcken, John S., 11, 64, 71, 73–74, **75**, 81–82, 92–93, 101, 105, 113–15, 122–24, 146, 149

Higgins, David W., 54–56, **57**, 59, 89–90, 105, 122–24, 126, 148

Howay, Frederick W., 127

Howe, Joseph, 18–19, **21**, 119, 150, 154n3 (chap. 3)

Hudson's Bay Company, 14, 63–65, 67, 76, 87, 107, 117, 147

Hume, David, 37

Humphreys, Thomas, B., 127

Imperial Act, 102–4

Kennedy, Arthur E., 92, 101–2

Kennedy, John F., 64–65

King, James, 40–41, **42**

King's Academy, 16

Leviathan (ship), 54–55, **65**

London Advertiser, 131

Macdonald, Sir John A., 132, 138

McClure, Leonard, 94, **96**, 97, 102–4

McCreight, John F., 119, **121**

Mormons, 29–31, 147

Mud Springs. *See* El Dorado

Muir, John, 64

Musgrave, Anthony, 105, 112–15, 117

Nagle, Jeremiah, 82

New Westminster, 93, 103–5, 146, 148

Novascotian, 17, 22–24

Oroville, 14, 49, **50**

Ottawa, 14, 51, 113, 116–17, 119–20, 124, 126, 129–33, 135–36, 146

Ottawa Citizen, 131, 146

Placerville, 14, 23–24, 32–33, 36–38, 41, 54–48

railways, 12, 91, 124, 128, 131–33, 135–39

Reform Convention, 108

responsible government, 12, 18–19, 63, 88, 101–2, 104, 114–16, 127, 131–32, 150

Rithet, Robert P., 147
Robson, John, 59, 104–5, **106**, 116–17
Ross Bay Cemetery, 11, **149**, 159n43
Rupert's Land, 107, 111–12

Sacramento, 14, 38, 40, **41**, 46, 154n3 (chap. 3)
Salt Lake City, 23, 28–32, 35, 37, 81, 147
Salt Spring Island, 85
San Francisco, 36, 41–42, 48–49, 54, 62, 70, 82–83, 97
Semiahmoo, 55
Seymour, Frederick, **56**, 107–8, **109**, 111–12
Smith, Charles McKeivers, 16, 25, 32, 47–51, 159n43
Smith, Charlotte E., 15
Smith, Jesse, 15
Smith, William A. *See* De Cosmos, Amor
Sproat, Gilbert M., 142–45

Taney, Roger B., 82
Texada Island, 56, 132
Thompson, John S., 17, 81

Trimble, James, 108
Trutch, Joseph W., 113, 117, 119
Tupper, Charles, 19

union of B.C. and Vancouver Island, 11, 80, 99–105,

Valentine, William, 17, 46
Victoria, 11, 12, 14, 28, 30, 53, **54**, 55–59, 61–65, 67, 69–70, 73–74, 76–77, 80–84, 86, 89–92, 97, 103–5, 108, 111–12, 115, 120, 122, 128, **129**, 133, 135, 138, 139, 143, 145–47, **149**
vigilante justice, 23–24

Waddington, Alfred P., 69–70, **71**
Walkem, George A., 136
Windsor, N.S., 14, 16
Workingman's Protective Association, 139
Work, John, 64

Yale, 54, 132
Yale Convention, 85, 110
Young, Brigham, 30